The Electric Kiln
A User's Manual

OTHER TITLES IN THE SERIES

THE ELECTRIC KILN

A User's Manual

Harry Fraser

A & C Black · London

University of Pennsylvania Press · Philadelphia

First published in Great Britain 1994
A & C Black (Publishers) Limited
35 Bedford Row
London WC1R 4JH

Reprinted 2000

ISBN 0-7136-5722-7

Published in 2000 in the USA by
University of Pennsylvania Press
4200 Pine Street
Philadelphia, PA 19104-4011

ISBN 0-8122-1758-6

Copyright © 1994 Harry Fraser

A CIP catalogue record for this book is available
from both the British Library and the U.S. Library
of Congress.

Cover illustrations
front Silver 565 top loading electric kiln by
Potclay Kilns Ltd.
back Teapot tile by Paul Scott.

Filmset in 10/12 Photina by August Filmsetting,
Haydock. Printed in Hong Kong

Contents

Introduction

Two major changes mark the evolution of the studio electric kiln in the UK. The first occurred gradually in a period of ten years or so in the late 1940s – early 1950s era. At that time, kiln manufacturers to the industry began to produce small-scale versions for a steadily increasing number of enquiries from specialist suppliers of pottery materials and equipment, from teachers engaged in the establishment of pottery departments in schools and from a growing number of craft potters. Many of these specialist suppliers – names such as Webcot, Podmore & Sons and Wengers spring to mind – have now disappeared but by making available suitably-sized electric kilns as well as a comprehensive range of materials and equipment they nurtured and helped develop the craft ceramics market into a very substantial activity over the following 30 years or so.

The second change occurred relatively suddenly. In 1980 the American dollar weakened against sterling, eventually bottoming out at about $2.40 to the pound sterling. It became economic to import to the UK some of the American top-loading kilns that were so widely used in their hobby ceramics market. Furthermore, due to economies of scale and the favourable exchange rate, these American kilns could be introduced to the UK (and other European markets) at prices which were very significantly lower than the production cost of the traditional front-loading electric kilns which were standard in the UK. Several thousand Olympic kilns and Amaco kilns, specially adapted to meet UK electrical safety regulations, were imported into the UK during the early 1980s. Importantly, these kilns featured a remarkable insulation brick which was a spin-off from the American space programme. This brick, the K23 brick, was imported by Moler Products in the UK and became the LW130 brick. It was quickly adopted by the UK kiln manufacturers who very quickly were forced to produce competitive top-loading kilns to survive.

Model 818 kiln (*Skutt Ceramic Products*)

Today, both top-loading and front-loading types are manufactured using bricks and ceramic fibre materials which thermally are vastly superior to the materials available in those early years. Although the American-style top-loading kiln remains the most popular type with craft users, especially hobbyists seeking small capacity kilns, there has been some resurgence in demand for traditional front-loading kilns but of course built with modern materials. This has been more noticeable with larger studio kilns in colleges and busy production situations where the more substantial construction, lower maintenance and longer life of the traditional front-loading type is more cost effective or preferred.

Electric kilns have several advantages over fuel-burning kilns. They are easy to operate and require relatively little skill: one needs only to adjust the switches at the right time and ensure that the firing is terminated at the appropriate point – and even this task can be dispensed with by fitting an automatic controller. Moreover, installation is easier and cheaper.

Electric kilns are also very safe to operate. If the kiln overfires, the heat is always confined to the firing chamber and the worst that can happen is damage to the ware load, the elements and the interior of the kiln. Electric firing also avoids the dangers involved in the burning of fuels. Such hazards can be minimised in fuel-burning kilns by sound design, correct installation and careful operation but these hazards need to be recognised and considered in those situations where the operation of the kiln is the province of someone perhaps not properly trained or sufficiently interested, as may happen in schools for example.

In view of these advantages it may seem surprising that the electric kiln has not completely replaced the fuel-burning kiln. The fact that it has not done so is due to two main reasons. One is the generally higher cost of firing. The other is that regular reduction firing is not a practical proposition in an electric kiln. If you want to make reduction-fired ceramics you need a gas, oil or wood-fired kiln, not an electric one. However,

The 32 cubic foot 'Big Olympic' kiln has a cantilevered lid which is spring-assisted for easy opening (*Olympic Kilns*)

Left
3 cubic foot front-loading kiln (*Potclays Ltd.*)

'Silver' S65 kiln fitted with extension ring to give 8.6 cubic foot capacity (*Potclays Ltd.*)

because of its simplicity, ease of operation, uniformity of firing and safety, the electric kiln is certain to remain easily the most popular way of firing studio ceramics.

The principle of the electric kiln is really quite simple. Electricity is applied to a resistive load (the elements) inside the kiln and radiant heat is generated as the resistors are energised. Heat is thereby transmitted to the ware load and is kept within the firing chamber of the kiln by insulation materials which line the walls, roof and base of the kiln. As the temperature climbs, some form of energy regulator is used to control the amount of electricity fed to the resistors and thus to control the rate of temperature increase.

However, this is a very simplistic view. A better knowledge of electric kilns can readily be gained by looking at their construction techniques and by having an awareness of the various accessories and correct method of use. By discussing these issues and contributory ones such as the effect of heat on ceramic materials; the control of firing temperature; kiln maintenance etc., a good understanding of the modern studio electric kiln and its correct operation and maintenance will be acquired.

Let us begin by looking at those factors which affect our choice of the most suitable kiln. To do this we first need to review the relative merits of the various kiln types and also to consider siting and electrical facilities because these may dictate limits on the size and type of kiln which can be accommodated.

'Firecraft' front-loading kiln (*Kilns & Furnaces Ltd.*)

Chapter One
Kiln Types

Top-loading kilns vs. Front-loading kilns

As the name implies, these are loaded from the top and they feature both lift-off and hinged lid types. It is more difficult to meet electrical safety regulations with lift-off lids and so the hinged lid is the norm. The American-style top loaders are relatively lightly constructed – usually with an outer case of stainless steel sheet or anodised aluminium – and a 75 mm thick wall made of K23 brick or K23 with 12 mm ceramic fibre back-up insulation. Some designs such as the Amaco Gold and Potclays Silver kilns feature separate base disc units enabling the base to be turned over and the opposite side used in the event of damage to one side. Some of these kilns can also be made larger or smaller by adding or detaching a section (see photograph on p. 42). Kilns may have one or several energy regulators to control firing speed. Those with several energy regulators, each controlling a different section of the kiln, enable the heat input to one section to be adjusted differently to the others and this can occasionally be useful.

There are some drawbacks. Their construction is generally much lighter and less robust than traditional front loaders and so they can be much more easily damaged by accidental collision. Lids are especially vulnerable since they generally are constructed of a cemented brick with a metal band around the periphery to keep everything clamped tightly. The lid brickwork itself is not otherwise supported and heavy weights placed on top (e.g. moulds for drying) will easily crack it through. Brick lids can be heavy to lift and some kilns have been fitted with fibre lids as an alternative. These generally have solved the weight problem but have introduced others. Frequently they sag into the firing chamber but also they occasionally tend to release particles of fibre during extended use which fall onto the pots below. The tips of ceramic fibres can partly convert to cristobalite which can be a health hazard in larger kiln installations. For these reasons, brick lids are usually preferred on studio electric kilns except where the size is so large that the lid weight would be impracticable. Even so, with large kilns it is possible to design a cantilever system (see photograph on p. 8).

Some top loaders are built to a much more robust standard with kiln walls of a similar thickness to traditional front loaders and with a similar angle-iron framework. Others are made structurally more durable by using heavier gauge sheet and more extensive cladding as well as thicker walls. Naturally however such kilns are more expensive than other top loaders and one of the principal advantages of top loaders over front loaders – that of price – may be marginal with this design.

Kilns with walls only $2\frac{1}{2}$ in. (63 mm) to 3 in. (76 mm) thick are fine for earthenware use (and brilliant for small-size kilns) but, dependent on the design of the kiln, there can be heat problems arising from high temperature (stoneware and porcelain) firings with larger kilns (above 10 cu. ft.) if fired on long schedules. Under these circumstances, excess heat passing through the kiln walls into switchboxes fitted to them can affect electrical controls such as energy regulators and contactors housed there, thus reducing their life expectancy. Indeed, this is a principal reason why maintenance costs on top loaders tend to be higher than on front loaders where the electrical connection and components are mounted in a large, relatively cool connection chamber at the rear of the kiln. To overcome this problem, it is important that the switchboxes fitted to the high-temperature kilns be well-ventilated and insulation or heat reflectors used where possible. Some designs have an open mesh housing for the switchbox and this allows good airflow but is electrically unacceptable in the UK. Others are designed with an air gap between the switchbox and the kiln. The Silver kiln from Potclays Ltd has a completely separate wall-mounting switchbox which removes any heat transfer problem but inevitably adds to the cost of the kiln. With this design, maintenance costs however are claimed to be similar to the front loaders.

The thin walls of the standard top loader allow the kiln to cool much more quickly and this can be an advantage in busy studios. Typically, a 6 cu. ft. kiln can be fired up to high earthenware temperatures and cooled down again in 24 hours, rendering it possible to fire every day. A kiln with, say, a $4\frac{1}{2}$ in. (115 mm) or 6 in. (153 mm) wall will fire up as quickly but will take a little longer to cool and one therefore cannot get the same number of firings each week – perhaps five instead of seven.

A further factor to be taken into account is that the exterior surface temperature of the typical 3 in. (76 mm) bricked top loader becomes hotter than boiling water on the metal sides and lid centre top on earthenware and especially high-temperature firings. The surface skin temperature can reach 140°–200°C under some firing conditions. This is not necessarily a problem but it does demand that combustibles be kept well away and also that children and especially handicapped persons be prevented from having contact with the kiln.

Top loaders take up less floor area than a front loader due to having an upward opening lid rather than a sideways opening door. The sectional top loaders in particular are useful for getting through narrow doorways, up flights of stairs etc. and generally for siting in locations which would be impossible for most other kilns (especially front loaders built in one unit). They are therefore useful and sometimes essential where space is very tight or in difficult access situations.

With top loaders one has the disadvantage of having to load and unload from the top. This means having to load and remove the kiln furniture as well as the ware with each firing. This is a nuisance and the larger-size kiln batts can be heavy: bending over the kiln to load and unload them can be a problem for people with back problems. The weight of the kiln lid can also be a difficulty. One advantage when loading from the top is that you have a good vantage point to see that pieces are not touching, particularly in the glaze fire. This advantage though has to be weighed against the risk of particles of grit or batt wash falling onto the pots below when the kiln batts are placed above them. Sectional top loaders have the added convenience of versatility of size, being easily made larger or smaller by addition or subtraction of a section. These sections may be of the blank, spacer ring type or multiple elemented extension rings (see figure on p. 33).

Advantages and disadvantages

The main advantages then of the top loader are lower initial cost, much better portability, ability to be sited in difficult access situations and they take up less floor space than front loaders.

The main disadvantages are lower durability, higher maintenance costs, greater heat emission and having to load and unload the kiln furniture as well as the ware each time.

Front-loading kilns confer the advantage of a much stronger construction. They last longer, are much more durable and resistant to the everyday knocks that can occur and their maintenance costs are significantly lower than most top loaders and especially so with larger kiln sizes. An advantage too is that the kiln furniture can be left in position and the ware therefore more easily loaded and unloaded.

Their major disadvantage is that they are invariably more expensive to buy and they lack the convenient portability of top loaders.

Other Kiln Types

Truck Kilns

With this type, the ware is placed onto trucks which run on rails. The trucks are loaded and unloaded from the kiln using either a turntable or, more usually, a 'transfer car' system which enables the trucks to be shunted to and from adjacent storage tracks.

25 cubic foot truck kiln (*Potclay Kilns Ltd.*)

It is an efficient system and particularly effective in the busy production department. When the kiln has been fired and has cooled to a temperature at which it is safe to open the door (normally below 200°C), the kiln door can be opened, the fired truck quickly removed and the door closed again to retain the residual heat of the kiln. The hot truck is then pushed along the rails to the transfer car which has been lined up to receive it and the transfer car, with its loaded truck, is then pushed to a shunt line. Here the hot, loaded truck is discharged and left to cool. From another shunt line a pre-loaded truck of ware is then moved onto the transfer car and conveyed to the kiln. The kiln door is quickly opened, the loaded car pushed into position and the door closed again.

In this way the kiln can be unloaded and recharged in a matter of a few minutes. This, allied to the fact that the kiln can be emptied before the ware has dropped to a temperature that permits handling, enables a very fast turn-round time to be achieved. Furthermore, retention of the residual heat in the kiln preheats the ware load thus reducing firing cost. Also, a stock of loaded kiln cars can be assembled in convenient time so that firings can be maintained at weekends or in holidays or other inconvenient times. For these reasons the truck kiln often offers the very best option for the busy semi-industrial pottery.

Sizes usually start from around 15 feet (4.6 m). Prices however are inevitably more expensive than other kiln types due to the extra cost of trucks, rail and the transfer system.

Trolley Kilns

The trolley is a similar concept to the truck kiln but the trucks run on rubber-tyred wheels on the floor instead of on rails. Usually the kiln has metal guides and rollers in the lower kiln walls to guide the truck into position, these acting against a metal strip running along the truck sides at bench level. More care has to be taken than with a truck kiln when loading trucks into the kiln and the ware is more susceptible to vibration from debris etc. on the floor but on the other hand the trucks can be moved anywhere provided the floor surface permits. Prices are similar or slightly cheaper than truck kilns.

Shuttle Kilns

A truck or trolley kiln that has a door at each end is called a shuttle kiln. A fired truck is removed from one end and a truck of unfired ware introduced at the other. When the fired truck is reloaded with ware, the sequence is reversed.

Moving Hood Kilns

With this type, the ware load is on a static platform or hearth and the kiln structure is moved into position over it. Frequently, the kiln is shuttled between two load settings exactly as a shuttle kiln except that the kiln is moved rather than the trucks.

Sliding Hearth Kilns

Here, the base of the kiln with its attached door can be slid forward on a short rail. The system is similar to a single drawer cabinet which is slid open to permit loading. It's a reasonable compromise between the higher cost but much better flexibility and efficiency of the truck kiln and the difficulty of loading the larger fixed-hearth kilns.

Top Hat Kilns

These employ the same principle as the moving hood kiln, the difference being that the kiln is placed into position from above instead of from the side. Like the moving hood and truck kiln types it has the advantage of enabling residual heat in the kiln to be retained for preheating the ware and it gives a quicker turn-round time. A gantry system is often used to transport the kiln from one load to another.

Sliding Hearth kiln (*Kilns & Furnaces Ltd.*)

Tunnel Kilns

Essentially an industrial concept, these are continuously-fired kilns used in larger factories. They lend themselves to flow-line production methods, trucks of loaded ware being loaded every hour or so into one end and removed from the other. A 'pusher' device gradually pushes the newly introduced truck – and a row of others in front of it – one truck length and then retracts to permit another load to be charged. The firing zone is at the centre of the tunnel and is maintained at temperature for months or years, or until maintenance forces a shutdown. Such kiln structures absorb a lot of heat in bringing up to temperature which is then wasted when the kiln is cooled: hence the need to keep them in continuous operation. Most tunnel kilns are gas-fired or oil-fired. However, developments in bricks and ceramic fibre (which have made it possible to massively reduce the amount of heat retained in the kiln structure) plus the very high capital cost of a tunnel kiln have made the type obsolete except in the largest concerns.

Roller Hearth Kilns

These are industrial furnaces which also are of continuous operation. The ware is placed directly on a bed of rollers or on batts running on the rollers which are driven and carry the ware through the kiln. The kiln is typically of very narrow height but wide, the single layer of ware receiving heat very efficiently from the roof or all-round and very rapid firing times can be achieved. Again the type is usually gas-fired and is restricted to industry because of its high investment cost.

There are various variations of the above but it is largely irrelevant to discuss them in a book such as this which is intended for the studio or semi-industrial user. It is hoped, however, that the brief comments above about the main 'other' kiln types is helpful in providing a better comprehension of what is achievable in the larger installations.

Truck of ware being placed into tunnel kiln for glost firing *Courtesy of Wedgwood*

Chapter Two
Kiln Selection, Siting and Electrical Considerations

Modern electric kilns provide a clean and safe way of firing wares at moderate cost. They are cheaper to buy than comparatively sized gas- or oil-fired kilns and with kilns smaller than about 6 feet (2 m) there will not be a great difference in firing cost – especially if off-peak electricity is used. The kiln is inevitably the most costly item of equipment for the potter and it is therefore important when selecting a kiln to consider all relevant factors so as to ensure that the right choice is made. Therefore, you need to consider all the circumstances surrounding your particular working and production conditions as well as your requirements. Unfortunately, there is no definitive checklist or formula for working out the right kiln for you. Your decision may well be a compromise between what you would really like and what you can afford, or have space/facilities for.

The major factors to take into account are these:

The approximate size of the kiln and the number of people using it.

The location of the kiln in terms of the available space and difficulty of access to the kiln site.

The electricity consumption of the kiln in relationship to the existing electricity supply.

The maximum temperature to which the kiln will be fired i.e. the type of ceramic wares to be produced.

Size and Capacity

You need to evaluate the size and quantity of pots that you wish to produce. This is very much more difficult to do than to state but it is a decision that only you can make. You will probably need to think in terms of firing your kiln about twice a week and that half of these will be biscuit and half glaze firings. Thus the kiln should be big enough to accommodate one week's production in one firing. In practice, this will leave some spare capacity but it is better to have this than a kiln which is too small. It may be of some help to know that kilns of up to 4 cu. ft. capacity tend to be popular with potters producing pottery as a hobby. Potters producing wares for some commercial gain tend to think in terms of 4 to 8 cu. ft. and sizes larger than this are increasingly for serious production needs. Schools tend to need kilns around 5 or 6 cu. ft. capacity but colleges usually require 10 to 15 cu. ft. and often several kilns. Obviously, the optimum size is influenced by the size of the ceramic items to be produced. Someone producing table lamps is going to need much more kiln space than someone producing jewellery for example, but the above generalisations hold true for a very wide range of wares.

Kiln Location and Access

All kilns give off an appreciable amount of heat during firing so space around and above the kiln must be allowed for. With front-loading kilns there should be sufficient space to allow a gap of at least 6 in. (15 cm) down one side and at least 18 in. (46 cm) down the other side to permit entry to the rear for servicing. Ideally, there should be a gap of at least 18 in. (46 cm) at the rear but this can be reduced to a minimum 6 in. (15 cm) provided that the kiln can be slid forward when servicing is needed. There should be at least a 30 in. (76.5 cm) space above the kiln. If, however, the walls or ceiling are of combustible materials then these minimum dimensions would need to be increased.

In the case of top loaders, a minimum of a 9 in. (23 cm) gap all round is essential and a gap of at least 36 in. (91 cm) would be needed above the kiln. Again, these minima would need to be increased if the walls or ceiling were of combustible materials.

A heat resistant board of about the same size as the top of the kiln can be mounted on 2 in. (5 cm) spacers below a combustible ceiling to give extra protection.

Adequate space is needed to allow for loading the kiln. Front loaders demand a little more floor space than top loaders for the door to swing open and for loading the kiln from the front. If floor space is very restricted, a top-loading kiln may be the only answer.

Front-loading kilns are normally manufactured as one complete unit which is relatively heavy and easily damaged if dropped even a few inches. The weight is such that special trucks may be needed to offload the kiln from the haulier's lorry and to transport the kiln to its final location. These trucks have difficulty in climbing steps, crossing lawns etc., or getting kilns through doorways which are narrower than the kiln! Consequently, it is important to consider how a kiln is to be delivered, and offloaded and moved to final position.

Skutt model 1027 kiln consists of three separate sections, each having an energy regulator. Separate base disc. (*Skutt Ceramic Products*)

It is therefore necessary to check the size of aperture of any doorway through which the kiln will have to pass. Most of the sectional top-loading kilns will pass through the narrowest doors, perhaps by turning the sections carefully on their side and carrying them through. Some manufacturers can specially build front-loading kilns in 'split-cabinet' form. These are built in two halves – enabling each half to pass through a much narrower gap – and then the two halves are bolted together on site. Kilns built in this way can also much more easily be taken up stairways, down cellar steps etc. A further alternative is to have the kiln actually built on site but this is very expensive due to engineer's time.

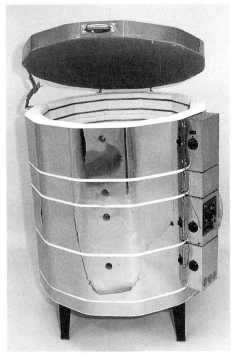

Sectional top loader with extension ring to top section. Three energy regulators. (*Olympic Kilns*)

The access route from the roadway should also be considered. Gateway widths, flights of steps, narrow footpaths with steeply sloping sides or retaining walls, soft ground or lawns to be crossed are some of the problems which can be encountered and which should be discussed with your supplier. Think about floor loadings also, particularly with a front-loading kiln. If the floor is wooden – and especially if your studio or workshop is upstairs – check to see that it will support the weight of the kiln. It may be

necessary to ensure that the kiln is positioned so that it spans the floor joists or to put down a steel sheet to spread the load of the kiln. With wooden floors, a heat resistant sheet may be required because radiant heat from some kilns may cause discolouration.

The ideal floor is one of concrete but whatever the floor material, it should be level. Even so, when the kiln is positioned it is best to check that it is mounted level and is evenly supported by the floor. If it is not level, it should be packed or shimmed level otherwise the kiln may undergo unnecessary stresses which could cause damage or distortion.

Ventilation

All kilns require some ventilation. A large electric kiln may well require a hood and an extractor system of some sort. This could be a wall-mounted fan or a kiln-mounted extraction unit such as the Orton Vent. With smaller kilns, opening windows sufficiently to allow a slight draft through the studio should suffice. Even a small top loader should not be used without some ventilation. *Never* fire a kiln in an area such as a closet or a cabinet where four sides are tightly enclosed. Air must be allowed to circulate around a kiln to prevent exterior overheating.

Electrical Requirements

Electrical power is measured in kilowatts, one kilowatt being 1000 watts. If the power consumption in kilowatts is known, and the electrical voltage is known, then one can calculate the current taken by the kiln. This is measured in amps and is determined by the formula Watts = Volts × Amps. Thus a 3120 watt (3.12 kW) kiln operating from 240 volts uses 13 amps.

Olympic 1214 kiln operates from 3.1 kW UK domestic power socket and fires to cone 10 (*Olympic Kilns*)

Kilns up to 3.12 kW can be fitted with a 13 amp, fused, three-pin plug and plugged into the UK domestic 240 volt power supply but power ratings larger than this demand that the kiln be wired in as one does with an electric cooker. A 7.2 kW kiln, for example, consumes 30 amps on full load from a 240 volt supply. In the UK, houses are usually fused to take up to 30 amps on the cooker circuit with often a further 30 amp fuse to a shower heater circuit. If these circuits are not in use it is therefore a simple matter to have the kiln wired to one of these fused outlets in the distribution board. 30 amps equates with a kiln of about 4 to 5 cu. ft. capacity and this is a popular size, perhaps partly because of the ease of wiring in.

The domestic distribution board is usually capable of handling larger kilns than this. Much depends, of course, upon the current consumed on the premises by other electrical appliances, The important thing is that the total current consumption at any one time must not exceed the capacity of the main fuse in the distribution board. This fuse is normally 100 amps but some older houses have 60 amps. The fuse is sealed and the only way you can tell is by looking at the rating stated on the meter or by asking the electricity board. Provided that electricity is not in use for cooking or heating, kilns of 12 kW or more can be installed into domestic premises. If the house fuse is 100 amps this still leaves 50 amps or so available for other appliances. Kilns of a rating larger than can be accommodated by the existing house supply will demand that extra power supplies be installed to the premises. This may or may not be expensive.

Local electricity boards are generally very helpful in advising what can be done in any particular situation.

The electricity supply cable from the distribution board or consumer unit to the kiln must be taken to a switchfuse unit or fused isolator mounted on the wall in a readily accessible position. This enables the kiln to be electrically isolated for safety and servicing. A suitably rated power cable is then used to make the 'hook up' from here to the kiln.

Single and Three Phase

Electricity is generated as three phase. Effectively, this is three separate power lines plus neutral which is then supplied along high voltage cables to transformers in towns and cities which reduce the cable voltage to manageable levels. In the UK this would normally be 240 volts between any one of these three power lines and neutral, but 415 volts if measured between any two of the three power lines. The three power lines and the neutral wire can often be seen strung along poles adjacent to roadways.

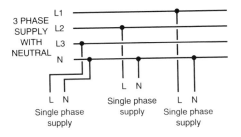

Figure 2.1 3 phase supply with single phase tappings

Builders of housing estates then take a single tapping to one of these three power lines (or 'phases') and also one to the neutral one and bring these two wires to a group of houses. A further connection to one of the two remaining phases and also the neutral will then be connected to another group of houses. The remaining third phase is then similarly connected to serve a further block of houses. Thus each house has a single phase supply made up of one of the three phase connecting wires plus neutral and of course the important earth wire.

It is desirable to keep the total demand on each of the three phase supply cables approximately equal. For this reason larger users of electricity may have tappings to all three phases brought to their distribution board from where single phase connections are taken to various parts of the premises. Large electrical appliances (such as medium and larger electrical kilns) can however be designed to be coupled to the three phase supply at the distribution board. This ensures that the appliance does not 'unbalance' the loading of the phases. It also gives some

economy in cable costs since a three phase cable is slightly cheaper than a similarly rated single phase cable. Importantly, it helps to ensure that the power supply to the kiln is better maintained. It does not however make any difference to the cost of firing: this is the same whether the kiln operates from single or three phase.

Firing Cost

Firing cost can be estimated by multiplying the kilowatt rating by the length of time the kiln is switched fully on and then multiplying this by the cost of one unit of electricity. Thus, if a 6 kW kiln is full on for say, four hours and half on for six hours (i.e. three hours full on), this is equivalent to seven hours full on. If we now multiply seven hours by 6 kW we arrive at 42 kW hours. This multiplied by the cost of one unit of electricity (currently 6.5 p in the UK) gives a firing cost of £2.73.

The cost of electrical power, however, varies to a large extent. In Scandinavian countries, for example, electricity is very cheap due to abundant hydroelectric power. In the UK it is possible to install off-peak electricity meters which allow electricity used in a seven hour slack demand period late at night and early morning, to be charged at about one-third daytime rate.

Firing Temperature

The temperature at which the kiln will be fired is also an important consideration. This is determined by the type of ware to be produced.

The elements used in kilns for the high temperature firing of stoneware and porcelain will often be very different from those used for, say, the low temperature firing of overglaze decorated ware. There are several different element types and, generally speaking, the higher the temperature to which the kiln will be fired, the more expensive the elements become.

Additionally, kilns designed for medium or low temperature work sometimes incorporate cheaper grades of refractory brickwork (and thereby cannot be converted to high temperature specification simply by fitting appropriate elements). Many kiln manufacturers however use the same high temperature refractories and downgrade only the elements. Ask the manufacturer if in doubt. The data plate on the kiln should incidentally indicate the designed maximum temperature.

It will be seen from the above that low temperature kilns should be somewhat cheaper than high temperature ones but a further important factor is that the power rating of the kiln is likely to be significantly lower with a low temperature kiln. A stoneware kiln will usually need about 20 per cent or so more power than a kiln designed for earthenware. If your power supply is very limited and you only need a kiln for earthenware use, you can therefore get a bigger kiln for the same power rating.

Elements are discussed in detail in Chapter 7.

Importance of Correct Voltage

Kilns are designed to operate from a definite voltage. A kiln designed to fire up to 1300°C from a 240 volt supply but coupled to a 220 volt supply may perform quite adequately up to earthenware temperatures but will struggle to reach much over 1200°C. It will almost certainly fall well short of its designed performance. It is possible to safeguard

against this by designing the kiln with extra kilowatts reserve power but this can give problems with cable sizes and component ratings and from the excessively fast speed at which the kiln then fires at the correct voltage. The voltage from which the kiln will operate is therefore important.

It is not generally appreciated that the voltage delivered to the kiln can vary with site conditions and location. Long cables lose volts. Thus a kiln positioned a considerable distance from the distribution board may receive a supply voltage which is significantly lower than that at the board itself. This is particularly true of the smaller diameter cables which, of course, have higher electrical resistance.

Heavy use of electricity by local workshops or by other departments in the same building can also cause a reduction in voltage. Sometimes the electricity board can switch you to another phase which is in less demand and thereby restore the voltage of your supply to a better level.

In the UK, the electricity supply authorities are required to deliver 230 volts + 10% − 6%. This means that the supply can be as low as 216.2 volts or as high as 253 volts and still be within tolerance as far as they are concerned. But with kilns that have a power rating just sufficient to enable them to reach the top temperature for which they are designed, a difference of only 10 volts can demand that differently rated elements be fitted to the kiln if it is to be consistently capable of reaching its top temperature.

Kilns are at their most efficient when first supplied. As firings are done, the elements gradually deteriorate and this

Hobbytech 40 kiln, 3.1 kW (*Cromartie Kilns Ltd.*)

'EP' 7.3 cubic foot 12 kW front loader (*Potclay Kilns Ltd.*)

causes a progressive increase in firing time and greater difficulty in reaching top temperature. If the effects of this gradual reduction in performance are to be minimised, it is obviously important to ensure as much as possible that the kiln is capable of performing to its fullest potential when first installed.

So, check the voltage of the supply at the point where the kiln is to be situated and if this is more than a few volts different from the normal supply voltage, speak to the kiln manufacturer who may need to amend the kiln element specification. If the supply cable has not yet been installed, your electrician or the kiln manufacturer could calculate the voltage at the kiln site if the exact voltage at the distribution board and the length of supply cable is known.

Incidentally, when firing a kiln it is often noticeable how much more slowly the kiln fires at peak periods of daytime use of electricity – especially at meal times in winter when heaters are also switched on. An advantage of off-peak electricity (in addition to the main one of being about one-third of the cost of daytime electricity) is that it is relatively free of such voltage fluctuations induced by other users.

Note
UK voltage specification used to be 240 volts ± 6% but this was changed to 230 volts in 1995. Other EC countries were also changed to 230 volts from 220 volts in order that this would eventually become the common voltage.

Chapter Three
Kiln Construction and Design

Framework

The framework of front-loading kilns is normally built of angle-section steel, although in smaller kilns the framework may be made from strip steel or pressed steel panels. Angle-section steel is, however, particularly useful as a basis for building since it gives support on two sides to the panels and brickwork. All joints are normally welded together but the sheet steel panelling can be fixed with screws or bolts. Sometimes, the larger panels are fixed only at one side or have oval slots to hold fixing screws down one side so as to allow for expansion which may otherwise cause a panel to bow outwards during firing.

9.5 cubic foot 'EP' kiln fitted with ventilated double-skin panels (*Potclay Kilns Ltd.*)

Instead of the usual single mild steel sheet panels, some front-loading kilns are now constructed with a double-skin for the door section and separate bolt-on, double skin panels on both sides of the kiln. These double skin sections are ventilated with louvres and the constantly moving stream of air through them keeps the outer skin at relatively low temperatures. Alternatively, the angle-iron framework is sometimes fitted with stainless steel panels for extra durability.

With small- and medium-sized kilns, it is becoming increasingly common to assemble the kiln from pressed steel panels without any metal cabinet frame.

Angle iron and sheet steel cabinet used as a base for a 6 cubic foot front-loading electric kiln

25

These undoubtedly look more attractive but do not have quite the same durability as kilns built with an angle-iron cabinet.

Front-loading kilns are usually built with an integral stand which allows for a compartment underneath the kiln hearth to take wiring and fitments to a front fascia panel. Similarly, a connection chamber is built usually at the rear of the kiln. With larger front loaders, connection chambers are sometimes built on the side of the kilns or all the electrical controls housed in a separate, free-standing panel.

Kiln Assembly

The construction of front-loading kilns involves building the cabinet first, followed by building in the insulation and

Top-loading kiln construction showing the 'Jubilee' screw fasteners securing the metal jacket around the brickwork of the kiln body, lid and base disc sections

refractory brickwork and finally adding the electrical fitments. This sequence is also followed with square section top-loading kilns using an angle-iron frame but with sectional, lightweight top-loading kilns, the sequence is different. Here, the brickwork is assembled first (and sometimes held in position with nylon or cord straps) and the metal skin – usually of stainless steel sheet – is then fitted around the brickwork and secured into position using Jubilee-type fasteners welded or pop rivetted to the metal sheet. The Jubilee clips can then be tightened to ensure that the whole assembly is securely clamped. The clips, incidentally, are normally hidden from view behind the switchbox which is added afterwards.

Where separate lid and base discs are used, these are assembled on an absolutely flat and level slab and, after final shaping, the stainless steel lid band is clamped around the assembly. Some lids however are built into a specially fabricated metal housing which covers the exterior surface.

With front loaders, the back-up insulation is of course placed into position first against the walls of the kiln. This may be in sheet form which makes things easy. Any intermediate insulation is then placed in position in front of this and finally the hot-face insulation is installed. It is often easier to install the base (hearth) and rear wall first. Plumb lines can then be pencilled down the rear wall at the intended joint with the side walls and these thus serve as a building guide.

Element grooves can easily be cut into bricks using grinding wheels mounted through an angled base and used like a circular saw. Powered clipper saws are used to cut and chamfer bricks on a production scale.

Brick cutting

Opinion differs as to whether it is best to fully cement, partly cement or to dry-joint the brickwork. What there can not be any argument about is that it is best to avoid any contact between the elements and the brick cement mortar. For this reason some kiln companies chamfer a rebate along two-thirds of the width of the edge face of the bricks which carry element grooves and apply the jointing cement only in this rebate. When these bricks are joined, they appear to be dry-jointed – as indeed they are at the hot face – but the rear two-thirds is cemented.

Vertically-mounted grinding wheel through slot in inclined bed is a simple way of forming element channels in hot-face bricks

Most companies completely cement the bricks together. When this is done, it is best to keep the joints between the bricks as tight as possible to reduce risk of elements being in contact with cement where they cross a joint. In walls which do not contain elements, the bricks are normally fully cemented but some people instead use ceramic paper as a gasket between the bricks. This has the advantage of allowing for some movement of the structure without the cracking of the bricks taking place as would happen if the bricks were cemented. It has the disadvantage that the reduced stability of the wall gives greater risk of some brick displacement during transit.

Hot-face brick slabs are widely used to span the top of the walls to form a roof. One problem is that these slabs are a maximum of 22 in. (56 cm) long. This means that they can only be used to span walls up to about 21 in. (54 cm) apart (allowing for about half an inch support by each wall). Beyond this it is necessary to form the roof in an arch which is structurally self-supporting. In that event, a former of curved ply or hardboard must be used to support the arch brickwork until the cement has properly set.

Roof slab positioned above side walls

Thick grade Kanthal wire is sometimes used to reinforce brick areas such as in the roof, the junction of walls with the roof and in the door to give added strength and resistance to movement. The wire is pushed into the brickwork like a skewer.

The repeated opening and closing of doors and lids presents greater risk of displacement and damage than in other parts of the kiln. The door brickwork is therefore usually keyed into the door frame by rebating the outer bricks to partly slot behind a channel section doorframe and the bricks inside these then cemented into place. Spyholes are drilled through the bricks from their predrilled positions in the front-door panel. Ceramic tubes to take the plugs are then often cemented into place and these serve to minimise the wearing effect of repeated use of the spy plug. Also, if the tube is extended through the steel door panel so that it extends $\frac{1}{8}$ in. (3 mm) or so, escaping gases tend to more easily clear the kiln instead of corroding the steel around each spyhole.

With top loaders, the lids are similarly rebated if the lid has a steel frame with a flange that the bricks can lock against. More usually, one relies on the outer stainless steel band being sufficiently tight to hold the structure under compression.

Doors are particularly difficult to shape so that they accurately fit the kiln opening. A layer of ceramic fibre can easily be glued to the face of the kiln brickwork or to the door brickwork to ensure an effective seal even though brick shaping is less than perfect. An accurately shaped door giving a close fit without the need for a ceramic fibre gasket all round its contact surface with the front of the kiln is likely to give a better seal in the longer term – and is a sign that the kiln is well constructed by people who know their job.

Rubber hammers and steel straight edges are used to ensure that brick assemblies are perfectly vertical, even and true. Flat rubbing stones are used to rub the brick surfaces level and to give a final trim.

There are several different brands of cement used to join bricks together and to fix fibre to bricks. Most of them consist of mixtures of molochite (calcined China clay) with China clay or ball clay and sodium silicate, with water added and the mix then blended to a cream consistency for trowelling. The cement should be thinly applied to brickwork to give the strongest bond and, after setting, the joint will invariably be stronger than the brickwork itself.

Some Design Considerations

Although electric kilns have several advantages over other types, one serious disadvantage is the size limitation. The performance of electric kilns falls away very rapidly if the width of the firing chamber exceeds about 30 in. (76.5 cm). Kilns of 20 to 26 in. (51–66 cm) across can be heated quite satisfactorily up to stoneware with elements in the hearth and two side walls only. Beyond this however, it becomes increasingly necessary to fit elements into the door and rear wall as well and above a 36 in. (89 cm) width it becomes very difficult to achieve a high-firing capability in reasonable time. The reason for this is that the ware load has to be heated entirely by radiation from elements in the walls of the kiln and the centre areas become too well-shielded or too far away.

A similar situation arises with top-loading kilns even though the elements are positioned all round the side walls (but not in the lid or base). A tall narrow

Heavy duty front-loading kiln with elements 'all around' and energy regulators dividing the elements into separate zones (*Cromartie Kilns Ltd.*)

kiln will always fire more quickly and to a higher temperature than a wider kiln of the same capacity and power rating. This is because the ratio of the heated surface area to the unheated surface area (lid and base) is higher in the narrower kiln and the centre areas are also closer to the elements.

One problem with tall, narrow kilns however is that they present greater difficulties in achieving temperature uniformity over a wide temperature range. When kilns are first heated, the energy is transmitted to the ware load by a combination of radiated and convected heat, plus a little conduction. At high temperatures however, virtually all the heat transmission is by radiation. At low temperatures, because convected hot air rises, the temperature at the top of the kiln quickly exceeds that of the bottom if all the elements are transmitting equal amounts of heat. This problem can be avoided in one of three ways. Firstly, the elements can be graded so that those at the top do not introduce as much heat as those at the bottom. This can work well but involves a lot of trial and error by the manufacturer and results in a further imbalance occurring if the kiln is used for a higher temperature firing. Secondly, the kiln can be fitted with separate energy regulators controlling the elements in the top and bottom of the kiln. For low-temperature firings, the energy input to the top of the kiln can be reduced by keeping the top energy regulator at a lower setting than the bottom one. This also works well but involves trial and error again, this time by the user, in achieving the right balance setting of the energy regulators. It does however enable balancing up to be done across the complete temperature range. This two-zone control method can, incidentally, be done automatically by a differential temperature control system (see Chapter 10). Thirdly, an Orton Vent extraction system can be fitted. This involves drawing in a small amount of air at the top of the kiln and exhausting it from the base via small holes drilled through the hearth or lower side walls. This has the advantage of removing any noxious gases from the kiln and kiln room and it does give more even firings. It is a real boon for decoration firings around 750°C but reduces the efficiency of the kiln slightly if used at high temperatures.

Power Rating

It is difficult to generalise about the number of kilowatts needed to power a kiln since this depends upon both the capacity of the kiln, the maximum temperature the kiln is to attain and the required firing speed. Kilns for fast firing or high temperature require a higher rating than others. A stoneware kiln for example may require 20 per cent more power than an earthenware one.

Kilns from various manufacturers nevertheless do tend to be rated with a similar number of kilowatts per cubic foot of kiln capacity although the ratio itself differs with kiln size. Small kilns for stoneware tend to have 2.5 to 3 kW per cubic foot dropping to about 1.5 kW per cubic foot for kilns about 10 cubic feet capacity.

If kilns are underpowered the results are obvious: the kiln will not reach temperature or be very slow in getting there. The consequences of having an overpowered kiln are less obvious. Installation costs may be a little higher because of thicker cables and where the electrical supply is restricted one may be forced to consider a kiln of smaller size than would be the case if the power rating of the kiln was lower. The speed of firing can be controlled by the energy regulator and so this is not a problem. What can be a problem with an overpowered kiln however is 'overshoot'. This means that the firing speed is so rapid when the kiln is being powered, that when it is switched temporarily off by the normal action of the energy regulator, the temperature continues to climb for quite a while before it falls back again. This can be an awkward problem with some decorating colours which are especially temperature sensitive and also with other materials which are being fired very near to their temperature limit. There are ways of minimising this with certain types of temperature controller (see Chapter 10) but suffice it to say that kilns can be problematic if they are either underpowered or overpowered.

Square section top-loading kiln (*Stanton Pottery Supplies*)

Figure 3.3 Exploded view: Amaco Excell electric kiln

DETAIL NO.	PART NO.	DESCRIPTION	PARTS/ KILN
1	24236T	Brick Lid W/O Band 10S	1
2	24237V	Bracket Lid Brace	2
3	24238W	Brace Lid Support Arm	1
4	N/A	Bracket Brace Support Arm	1
5	24240D	Brick Peep Hole Grooved 10S	6
6	24241E	Plug Peep	6
7	24242F	Brick Grooved Straight 10S	48
8	24243G	Brick Terminal Grooved 10S	5
9	24244H	Insulator Tubes	12
10	24245J	Shield Switch Box	2
11	28068C	Inf Switch 240/208	6
12	24246K	Box Switch Upper	1
13	28128E	Knob Switch Inf	6
14	24247L	Receptacle Male	2
15	24248M	Receptacle Female	2
16	24273E	Kiln Setter W/Timer (K Model)	1
17	24249N	Light Pilot	1
18	24274F	Box Master Switch	1
19	28071F	Connector 10 U	12
20	24275G	Shield Master Switch	1
21	24251R	Brick Grooved Kiln Setter 10S	1
22	24252S	Connector Supply Cord	1
23	24253T	Cord Power Supply Set	1
24	24254V	Stand Kiln 10S	1
25	24255W	Band S.S. Btm (Same as 35) 10S	1
26	24256X	Shield Heat Supply Cord	1
27	24257A	Slab Btm (Lid) 10S	1
28	24258B	Sash Lock	2
29	24259C	S.S. Body Band 10S	6
30	N/A	Elements (See Element Chart)	
31	24260M	Handles Section	6
32	24261N	Hinge Body Leaf R/L (Set) 10S	1
33	24262P	Hinge Rods (Set of Three) 10S	1
34	24263R	Hinge Lid Leaf R/L (Set) 10S	1
35	24255W	Band S.S Lid (Same as 25) 10S	1
36	24265T	Handle Lid	1
37	24266V	Box Switch Lower	1

ELEMENT CHART

EX-270			
38, 39	24002C	Top or Btm Element Coil 240 V	6
38, 39	24003D	Center Element Coil 240 V	6
38. 39	24004E	Top or Btm Element Coil 208 V, 1 Phase or 3 Phase	6
38, 39	24005F	Center Element Coil 208 V	6
38, 39	24006G	Center Element Coil 208 V, 3 Phase	6
EX-365			
38, 39	24017V	Top or Btm Element Coil 240 V	6
38, 39	24018W	Center Element Coil 240 V	6
38, 39	24019X	Top or Btm Element Coil 208 V	6
38, 39	24020Y	Center Element Coil 208 V	6
1	24267W	Brick Lid W/O Band 3" 10S	1
5	24268X	Brick Peep Hole Grooved 3" 10S	6
7	24269A	Brick Grooved Straight 3" 10S	48
8	24270B	Brick Terminal Grooved 3" 10S	5
21	24271C	Brick Kiln Setter Grooved 3" 10S	1
27	24272D	Slab Btm Lid 3" 10S	1

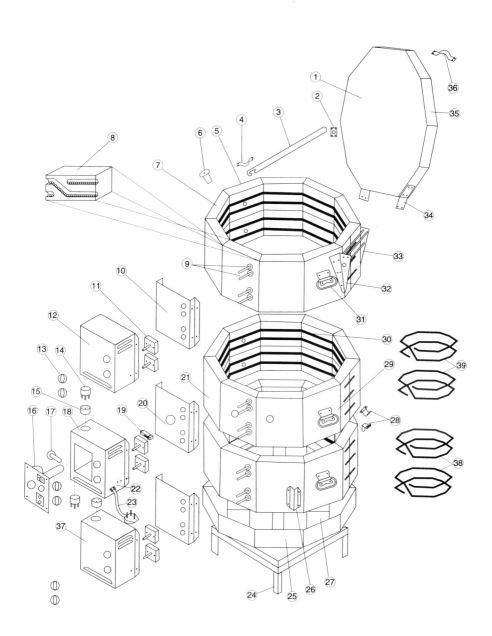

33

Chapter Four
Refractories and Insulation

In recent years the most significant advance in kiln technology has been the progressive development of high-temperature insulating refractory bricks. The bricks now generally used for hot-face installations are a spin-off from the American space programme which developed the heat-resistant tiles for the Space Shuttle. Allied to this has been the development of ceramic fibre which is of ultra-light weight and has very low thermal mass.

Refractory Insulation Bricks

The refractory insulation bricks generally used in the construction of studio electric kilns are of two types. Firstly, we have the type referred to as 'HTI' or 'High Temperature Insulating' brick. This has become a generic term for bricks of similar quality and performance from different manufacturing sources such as the HT1 (Steetley Refractories), Moler 25 (Moler Products) and HR140 (Hepworth

Ceramic fibre, grooved K23, K23 and HTI hot-face bricks

Refractories). The HTI brick is a white, porous brick which is easily cut and shaped and has good insulating properties. It has a service classification temperature of 1400°C.

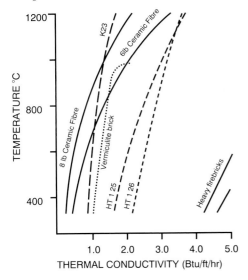

Figure 4.1 Relative insulation values of ceramic fibres and bricks

For hot-face installations however, these bricks have largely been replaced by the second type of brick which is the K23 brick manufactured in the USA by Babcock & Wilcox, now Thermal Ceramics Ltd. The K23 brick has excellent insulation properties and is thermally much superior to the HTI type (and even superior to ceramic fibre above 1000°C) but has the disadvantage of being much more easily compressible. For this reason the HTI brick, being harder and more durable, continues to be used around door closing surfaces and in any locations where slight abrasion or compression may take place. The K23 also has a lower service temperature than the HTI but can be used up to 1300°C. Beyond this temperature, higher grade bricks (K26, HR155 etc.) are available but are not normally needed in studio electric

furnaces. The very high porosity of both brick types makes them easy to cut with a normal hacksaw. They can be very easily worked and boring holes or shaping element channels in them is simple to do.

Ceramic Fibre

Ceramic fibre is a remarkable insulation material. It is produced by melting an alumino-silicate material in an electric arc furnace at a temperature between 1850°C and 1950°C. The molten material is then divided into fibres either by a blast-drawing technique using compressed air or by spinning the melt on rotating discs (which produce fibres exactly as candy floss is produced). It is a remarkable insulant but, in fact, at temperatures above 1000°C the modern K23 brick is actually superior in thermal properties (see Figure 4.1). For this reason – but mainly the fact that ceramic fibre is not load-bearing and will not support the weight of elements – bricks are generally preferred as the hot-face lining for high-temperature studio kilns. Where ceramic fibre is used as the hot-face lining, it is usual to use HTI brickwork as corner posts in the firing chamber. The elements are then supported by rods passed through them or by special refractory element carriers which are fitted between and carried by the corner posts.

The extremely low thermal mass characteristics of ceramic fibre result in a rapid cooling rate and, provided the ware load can withstand it, quick turn-round times are possible. It is not unusual for example, for ceramic fibre-lined decorating kilns to be fired to 750°C and cooled three times per day.

Ceramic fibre can be formed into paper, blanket or board and is available in different densities of which the two most common are 'low density' (96 kg/m) and

Checking level: truck kiln wall construction

'high density' (128 kg/m). Each of these two grades are available in two service temperature grades of 1260° and 1400°C. The higher temperature grade includes a mullite addition which gives better resistance to attack by glaze vapours.

One problem with ceramic fibre, particularly when used for lids of top loaders, is that in time the tips of the fibres partly convert to cristobalite and become more brittle. They sometimes break away and can fall onto ware underneath. Because of the fibrous nature of ceramic fibre and the possible presence of cristobalite after extended firing, the removal and replacement of ceramic fibre in an industrial situation is a health risk which demands the wearing of respirators (see page 120).

Ceramic fibre blanket is very commonly used in $\frac{1}{2}$ in. (13 mm) thick blanket form as a back-up insulant to K23 bricks. Many top loaders have this construction, especially where the brickwork is dry-jointed, the blanket continuing to provide a seal when the brick joints become less than perfect after extensive firing.

Back-up Insulation Materials

There are a variety of back-up insulation materials including calcium silicate slabs and bricks, diatomaceous earth types, vermiculite, glass fibre, mineral wool etc. The most commonly used material is calcium silicate slab which is produced in two grades: 950°C and 1100°C and both are excellent insulation materials which can easily be cut and shaped.

Mention must also be made of an exceptionally good insulating material called Microtherm. This finds use in aircraft to insulate the heat of jet engines and is available in precut sheets which are enclosed in a net material. When compared to other insulants of similar thickness, it initially appears to be expensive but it is correspondingly more efficient. Thus, it finds particular use in situations where both insulation and space saving are important. It seems certain that Microtherm will become more widely used in ceramic kilns wherever there is a need to reduce the thickness of insulation without reducing thermal efficiency.

Mortars and Cements

Strictly speaking, mortars are used to join bricks and slabs together as in the construction of kiln walls whereas cements are used to form castables for the production of special shapes. Nevertheless the term 'cement' is increasingly being used in connection with mortars and terms such as 'cement mortar' or 'jointing cement' are often encountered. In kiln building, the word 'cement' has therefore become a generic term to include mortars.

Cements and mortars are broadly similar compositions generally based on aluminous clays with a sodium silicate binder but cements usually contain

aggregates such as crushed brick, Molochite, exfoliated vermiculite etc. or mineral wool, whereas mortars are smoother compositions that enable fine joints to be obtained. Cements are little used in studio electric kilns but mortars are extensively used to bond together hot-face and back-up brickwork to form a stable and gas-tight structure.

Mortars (and cements) are available in both air-setting and heat-setting types. Some of these are designed for application to a dampened surface but the ones most commonly and conveniently used are for application to dry brickwork only. Some mortars are in powdered form and require water addition to prepare them for use; others are ready mixed.

Whichever the mortar, it is important to use only clean water, to mix well into a creamy consistency and to use thin joints when assembling brickwork. A thin coat of mortar can also be used to secure fibre to brickwork as when fixing a ceramic fibre gasket as a door seal.

Care should be taken to avoid or at least minimise any contact between elements and cements or mortars as this can shorten element life.

After firing, the cemented joint between bricks is invariably stronger than the bricks themselves.

Chapter Five
Kiln Controls and Accessories

Whatever the kiln, we need to be able to control the firing speed and we need to be able to shut it off at the right temperature. We will likely also need to 'soak' i.e. hold the temperature for a while at the required temperature. Manually-operated switches are invariably fitted to enable these things to be done but it may be preferred to do these things automatically with a suitable control instrument. There are a variety of temperature controllers available ranging from those which just provide temperature cut-off to some which provide very sophisticated control over the complete firing cycle. Many potters will however elect to manage using a simple temperature indicator, controlling firing speed manually with the energy regulators and manually switching off at the required temperature indicated by the pyrometer or by the collapse of cones.

Kiln Controls

Venting

Additionally, we need some method of enabling moisture and combustion products to escape during the early stages of a firing. This is usually done by having a removable vent plug in the top of the kiln or perhaps a series of spyholes in the side or front of the kiln which have the dual purpose of enabling the inside of the kiln to be viewed and also acting as ventilation ports. It is however possible to ventilate the kiln automatically by fitting an automatic damper in the roof of the kiln. This is left open at the start of the firing and is then driven closed by the action of a reversing motor actuated by the temperature controller at a particular point, or by a time switch at a particular time in the firing. Such automatic dampers are expensive and therefore are normally encountered only in large kilns in semi-industrial situations. For most studio potters, manual insertion of the

Automatic damper operated by reversing motor mounted on the top of a front-loading kiln and controlled by a time switch mounted on the side of the kiln above the two energy regulators

vent plug part way through the firing is no problem and an inconvenience readily accepted in light of the cost of the automated alternative. In the USA it is common practice with top-loading kilns to slightly prop open the kiln lid for ventilation purposes when firing. This can not be done in the UK due to electrical regulations which demand that power be shut off from the kiln if the lid is lifted.

Energy Regulators

It is a characteristic of all kilns that they fire progressively slower as temperature increases. If a kiln is to be capable of reaching in reasonable time even the lowest temperatures to which ceramicists fire, the firing speed at the start will be too rapid. (See Figure 5.1.) Some method of controlling firing speed is therefore essential.

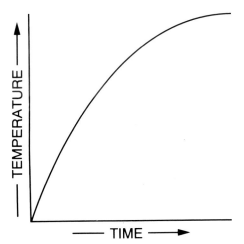

Figure 5.1 Firing speed with energy regulators full-on

Such controls are of three types. Firstly, one can have a series of simple on-off switches, each controlling one or more elements. As the temperature climbs, more of the switches are switched on to maintain firing speed. Alternatively, there is a rotary switch which can be clicked to off, low, medium and high positions. These energy regulator switches, commonly called 'series/parallel' switches (because they switch the elements either into a series or into a parallel circuit), are simple to use but are less popular than the third type of switch which is infinitely adjustable.

Energy regulators. The two at the bottom show side view and without their control knobs

These infinitely adjustable energy regulator switches have a graduated scale ranging from off to full-on. Some have a scale graduated from 0 to 100 and are sometimes referred to as 'percentage switches' because the switch position approximately indicates the percentage of time the switch allows current to be fed to the kiln. At a setting of 40 for example, the current would be switched on for 40 per cent of the time and switched off for 60 per cent. They can be heard carrying out this switching action. Typically you hear a click and a humming noise as power is fed to the elements, then a click as the power is cut off. The time interval that the power is off gradually diminishes as the switch is moved to higher positions and cycling eventually ceases at or near the full-on position.

These energy regulators are sometimes called 'Sunvics' (after a company of that name which supplied several kiln companies with this type of switch). 'Simmerstat' is another name commonly used in the UK and 'Infinite Switch' in the USA.

The switching action of many of them however is not very linear in that 20 or 30 per cent of their action occurs in the first half of the switch movement and the remaining 70 or 80 per cent in the final half. Furthermore they tend to slightly differ from switch to switch so that the switching action of a replacement may not be exactly the same as the original. By contrast, some of the electronic types of energy regulator are very accurate and predictable.

Energy regulators are only capable of switching up to a maximum of about 16 amps (and very much less than this for the electronic types). This is about the current drawn by a 240 volt kiln rated about 3.8 kW – which will be quite a small kiln. Larger kilns than this either must be fitted with extra energy regulators, each one independently controlling a number of elements which collectively draw less than 16 amps, or the energy regulator must be made to drive a heavier duty electrical relay or contactor which itself switches the full power to the kiln when energised by the energy regulator.

The life of energy regulators is significantly longer when they only have to switch a small current to a contactor instead of having to carry the full power to elements.

Electrical Contactors

As mentioned above, these are used to feed heavy electrical current to the kiln. They can be considered to be like a valve in a water pipe. When it is necessary to stop the flow of water (electricity), the valve (contactor) is turned (switched) off and when the flow is again required, it is turned on again. Switching on is done by energising a small electromagnet in the base of the contactor. This magnet attracts a metal link which is pulled against the action of springs and bridges sets of contacts. One contact in each set of contacts receives the incoming power supply, the other takes the supply onwards to the kiln element circuits. When the electromagnet – which incidentally is known as the 'holding coil' – is de-energised, the springs force the contacts apart and the power supply to the elements is broken.

The holding coil receives its signal either from an energy regulator or from a temperature controller. Although some energy regulators can carry up to 16 amps – enough to power a very small kiln, temperature controllers invariably cannot handle more than a very few amps. Whenever a temperature controller is installed onto a kiln it is therefore necessary to also install a contactor if the kiln circuitry does not already have one.

Electrical contactor

Safety Isolation Switches

In the UK and several other countries, it is no longer permitted to supply kilns which do not have a means of automatically cutting off the power supply to the kiln elements when the door or lid is opened. Moreover, this has to be done in a fail-safe way using a device which switches the full electrical load of the kiln. One cannot use a contactor for this because these use springs to break the supply and should these fail or the contactor points weld themselves together, the contactor would continue to feed power to the element circuits. Consequently, a positively-acting switch or a trapped-key system has to be used.

Positively-acting switches generally consist of a heavy duty rotary switch which is mounted behind a fascia panel on front loaders, or inside the switchbox on top loaders. A spindle with a handwheel at one end and a box spanner at the other and which is securely fitted to the lid or door of the kiln is then engaged with the squared shaft of the switch when the lid or door of the kiln is closed. Turning the spindle through 90 degrees then activates the switch and at the same time prevents the spindle from being withdrawn due to the rectangular shape of the box spanner being locked behind the fascia panel. To open the door one has firstly to turn the spindle back through 90 degrees to enable it to be withdrawn from the fascia and this action, of course, turns off the power at the switch.

In some smaller kilns there are heavy duty switches operated by a plunger which is depressed as soon as the lid is opened. Here the switch is arranged so that current flows when the switch plunger is extended. When it is depressed against the action of springs, the current is switched off. Should the springs fail it will remain in its off mode.

Whatever the switch system, it has to be designed so that it can not easily be defeated by the insertion of probes etc.

Trapped-key interlock systems which involve a key-operated electrical isolator on the kiln or fixed to a nearby wall are also widely used. The key can only be withdrawn from the isolator when the power is switched off: in the 'on' position, the key is trapped in position. This key is the only key which fits a key lock on the door of the kiln. When the door is properly closed, the key can be inserted and turned to securely lock the door in position. The door can then only be opened by turning the key to release the lock but it is then trapped and cannot be withdrawn. Thus the key is trapped either in the door lock when the door is open, or in the electrical isolator when the power is switched on. It is therefore impossible to have the power on and the door open at the same time.

Such trapped-key switch systems are often called Castell Interlocks but this merely reflects the trade name of one manufacturer and there are various others.

Fitment of safety isolation switches renders it impossible to vent a top-loading kiln during firing by propping the lid open as is so commonly done in the USA and elsewhere. This is why most UK top loaders additionally have a vent in the lid as well as the usual ones in the side of the kiln.

Power-on Light

A red power-on indicator light showing that power is being supplied to the kiln from the supply cable is a mandatory requirement in the UK. To comply with these regulations it is usually arranged that a red light on the kiln illuminates as soon as power is switched on from the

The spyhole plugs in the side and the vent plug in the lid of these 'Silver' top-loading kilns can clearly be seen. Also noticeable is the handwheel actuated safety switch extending above the lid. The larger kiln, incidentally, has a detachable intermediate section enabling the kiln to be altered in size. (*Potclays Ltd.*)

wall-mounted isolator to the kiln. Some lights however are wired from the output side of the kiln isolator or safety switch, or from the output side of a Kiln Sitter so that they illuminate when power is fed from this initial switch to the kiln circuits. In this event there should always be an additional power-on light installed on the kiln or prominently nearby to denote that power is being fed from the wall isolator.

Additional lights – usually amber or white in colour – are also often installed into switchboxes or control panels to denote the functioning of various accessories. They are, for example, occasionally used in conjunction with energy regulators or temperature controllers to indicate when they are operating.

Kiln Accessories

Time Switches

There are a variety of time switches differing in size and complexity. Some temperature controllers have built-in, electronic time switches to provide a delay-on and/or emergency shut-off facility and this is discussed in more detail in Chapter 10. Here we will be more concerned with time switches installed as separate units on the kiln, or wall-mounted.

Generally such time switches are fitted with a scale graduated in 24-hourly divisions, each division usually being subdivided into portions of one hour. Movable pointers are fitted into numerous holes drilled around the periphery of the scale. In this way, various on and off times can be programmed. Many time switches also have a day facility so that operation of the kiln can be confined or planned for certain days of the week.

The time taken for a firing will vary dependent upon various factors and consequently it is not advisable to use a time switch to control the firing point. They can however be useful to automatically switch on the kiln at inconvenient times – perhaps early in the morning – enabling the firing then to be completed during the normal day. More commonly, they are used as an emergency shut-off device, being set to automatically switch off an hour or two after the time a firing should have been terminated by the action of a temperature controller or, indeed, manually by the operator. To do this they are usually wired in series with the electrical supply to the energy regulator and contactor holding coil circuit.

A Limit Timer device is often fitted to a Kiln Sitter. This is a 20-hour timer which has to be set for the maximum permissible number of hours firing time after which it will automatically switch off the kiln. If a kiln firing normally takes about 10 hours then one might set the Limit Timer for, say 11 or 12 hours to ensure emergency shut-off in the unlikely event of the Kiln Sitter failing to do so.

Heat Fuse

These are of two types: the fusible link and the electronic, resettable variety. The fusible link type looks very much like a thermocouple and is inserted into the kiln through the wall or roof exactly as one would with a thermocouple. Inside the porcelain sheath of the heat fuse are two wires which are joined at their tip by a temperature sensitive alloy which suddenly melts when that temperature is reached. In doing so, it open-circuits the wires and since the heat fuse is installed in series with ancillary supply to the contactor holding coil, the kiln cannot continue firing and cools down. The fusible link temperature is available in alternative 50°C increments but in kilns firing up to 1300°C is normally selected for a temperature of 1350°C. Sometimes heat fuses rated at 1300°C are fitted and 'fail' during normal stoneware firings to 1260°–1280°C. This is almost always because the position of the heat fuse coincides with a hot spot or the temperature indicated for the firing is actually higher than it is believed to be. Fusible link heat fuses are generally extremely accurate in their activating temperature.

The problem with this type of heat fuse is that the cost of a replacement element is appreciable and one is needed if the fusible link melts. Nevertheless, this is very much cheaper than the extra damage that would otherwise be caused to the kiln if the kiln temperature continued to climb until the elements and ware load collapsed.

Resettable heat fuses have the advantage that they can be reset by the touch of a button. They operate by measuring the millivoltage generated by a thermocouple and convert this into degrees Celsius (centigrade) – exactly as does a temperature indicator. If the received signal is equivalent to the trip temperature of the heat fuse, then the ancillary supply circuit to the contactor is open-circuited by the heat fuse to switch off the kiln.

Resettable heat fuse

Some resettable heat fuses have selectable alternative trip temperatures; others are for a single fixed temperature. Most can operate from the same thermocouple provided for a temperature controller but a separate thermocouple is needed in some circuits.

The electronic heat fuse is therefore similar to a simple cut-off temperature controller and it is subject to the same risk of some error occurring in the signal generated by the thermocouple as can happen with any temperature controller or temperature indicator. These risks are discussed in Chapter 9 but suffice it to say

that system errors result in the electronic resettable heat fuse being not quite as accurate as the fusible link types. Nevertheless, if well designed and carefully installed they function with good accuracy and are preferable to the fusible link type because of the ease with which they can be reset.

Some temperature controllers, e.g. the Firemaster type, have a built-in electronic heat fuse operating from an independent circuit within the instrument. It is set to trigger at about 1325°C and automatically resets when the instrument is programmed for its next firing.

Ventilation Systems

There is no doubt that some noxious gases are generated during the firing of ceramic glazes and decorative colours. The gases generated by biscuit firings are somewhat less noxious but are given off in greater volume. They consist largely of water vapour arising from the dissociation of clays and other minerals mixed with traces of a variety of harmful materials. These are discussed more fully in Chapters 13 and 19; here we are concerned only with means of their removal.

The Orton Vent and Skutt Environvent systems are devices which draw a small volume of air into the top of the kiln to replace a similar amount drawn out of the base by the action of an extraction fan, usually positioned immediately underneath the kiln. Small holes have to be drilled in the top and base of the kiln but this is easily done using the templates provided. They were originally designed for top-loading kilns but versions are available for coupling with front-loading kilns, the extraction unit being mounted on the side of the kiln or on a nearby wall. Since the small amount of hot air

Orton Vent complete with stand for top-loading kilns

extracted is diluted by a much larger amount of cool air, the exhaust from the system is relatively cool and easily ducted away to outside atmosphere.

An alternative is to have a ventilation canopy mounted above the kiln. The Vent a Kiln system has a spun aluminium canopy which can be raised or lowered over the kiln by a simple pulley system. Attached to the canopy is a low-powered fan extractor unit which draws air through the canopy to a flexible duct which should be routed to discharge to outside atmosphere. The unit operates very much like a cooker hood.

Both systems are effective in clearing away the fumes which emanate from all firings.

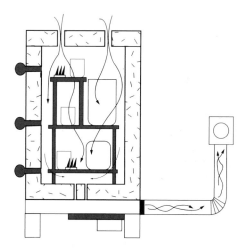

Figure 5.2 Orton and Skutt vent systems

45

The Vent a Kiln is a complete system including motorised fan with on/off switch, hood, convenient overhead counterweight pulley system and venting hose

Extension Rings

With some top-loading kilns, e.g. Skutt, Amaco and Potclays Silver models, it is possible to fit a separate kiln ring or section to increase the firing chamber capacity. These may be 'spacer' rings which do not have elements fitted, or 'heated' rings which are elemented and usually powered via a fitted cable and plug which fits a special socket on the kiln switchbox. Alternatively, a heated ring can be powered independently (usually from a domestic power socket) but one then has to manually switch off the section when firing is completed.

Spacer rings can be used to increase the size of the kiln for biscuit and other low-temperature firings but the extra kiln capacity generally results in unacceptable slowing in high-temperature firings.

Kiln Furniture and Temperature Controllers etc.

Kiln furniture to support the ware load is, of course, an essential 'extra' with any kiln rather than an optional accessory and therefore should not be considered in this section. You should ensure that you have the right thickness of shelves, that they are of the right size to allow sufficient airflow between the shelf and the kiln wall, and that you have a sufficient number and variety of props to give a stable assembly and allow for flexibility in shelf positioning. There is much to discuss about kiln furniture and a separate section is therefore devoted to this topic in Chapter 11; similarly with temperature indicators and control instruments, which are covered in Chapters 9 and 10.

Chapter Six
Wiring the Kiln

The need to install a switch fuse unit or fused isolator on the wall has previously been mentioned. Once the internal wiring of the kiln has been completed, a suitable power cable is connected and the final stage is to make the connection of this supply cable to the wall isolator or switch fuse unit. But first let us look at the internal wiring of the kiln.

Mains power connection terminals will usually be provided in the switchbox or connection chamber of the kiln and should be clearly labelled L or Line, N or Neutral, and E or Earth (ground). If the kiln is also suitable for three phase operation then there will instead of one be three line terminals (labelled L1, L2 and L3 respectively). If, as is usual, the three phase supply is treated as three single phases, each wired to neutral, then such three phase kilns can easily be converted to single phase by connecting a strapping wire between L1, L2 and L3 and making a single phase connection. This is very common practice. A three phase supply supplied without a neutral (delta configuration) demands a completely different wiring arrangement to the elements and it is not possible to convert such three phase kilns to single phase without extensive rewiring.

Wiring is typically arranged so that from the connector block which receives the incoming power supply, the kiln is wired to the safety isolator switch and from there to the input side of the contactor. From the output side of the contactor, wiring is taken directly to the elements. The contactor is controlled by an energy regulator or temperature controller which receives its power from a separate 1.5 mm wire taken from the incoming supply at the mains connection terminals or isolation switch. This separate power supply is called the 'auxiliary', 'secondary' or 'ancillary' circuit and should be taken to a 3 amp fuse normally mounted on the fascia panel or switchbox. From the fuse the supply is taken to the energy regulator or temperature controller which controls the contactor holding coil (see Figure 6.1).

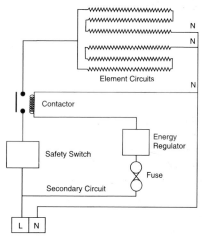

Figure 6.1 Typical schematic wiring arrangement of safety switch and contactor, the latter controlled by an energy regulator in the secondary circuit. There are three elements in series in each of two element circuits in this example.

If the kiln is wired into separate zones, then a further energy regulator and contactor is needed wherever the current taken by a zone exceeds 13 to 15 amps. If it does not exceed this, then the power to the elements in that zone can be taken through the energy regulator instead of to a contactor. This is illustrated by Figure 6.2 which shows two ways of wiring the power to the elements, one using a contactor to switch the total load and the alternative of using several energy regulators each carrying a portion of the total electrical load and each serving a few elements.

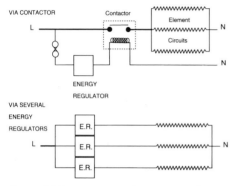

Figure 6.2 Two ways to wire power to the elements

Note however that the life of energy regulators is much reduced if they switch current directly to the kiln elements and thus are carrying electrical loads approaching the limit of their designed capability. The ideal way is to have the energy regulators controlling contactors which carry the load rather than the load being carried by the regulators themselves. The Silver S105 kiln (Potclay Kilns Ltd) is made this way. Although it has three energy regulators, each one of these controls a contactor which switches electrical supply to an element zone. Since the kiln is rated at 15 kW the contactor to each zone switches 5 kW. An alternative method of wiring this kiln would be to divide each of the three element zones

into two and then to fit six energy regulators, each switching 2.5 kW directly i.e. without use of contactors.

Contactor Wiring

Contactors usually have three or four contacts or 'poles' to which connections can be made. A 6 kW contactor with three poles can carry 2 kW per pole.

Contactors can be rated either as the total current they can take per pole or alternatively the total current, assuming this is divided equally per pole. It is important to know the difference. If you wire a 7 kW kiln to one pole of a contactor rated to carry 7 kW over its three poles, it will of course rapidly fail unless loop connections are made to the other two poles so that the load is spread or shared over three poles rather than one. With a single phase supply therefore, either wire the power to a large contactor which is capable of carrying the full current of the kiln on one pole or connect to the centre pole of three poles and make a loop connection from there to each outer pole. (See Figure 6.3.)

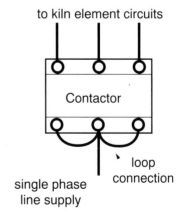

Figure 6.3 Contactor wiring

As previously mentioned, it is common to treat a three phase supply as three

48

single phases and to wire each phase to a separate pole on the contactor. An energy regulator or temperature controller is then used to control the switching of the contactor holding coil thus switching all three phases onwards to the kiln elements.

Element Connections

The power supply from the output side of the contactor is fed directly to the elements. The connections to the elements must be firmly made using a connector which is of reasonable size and strength to ensure good contact with the element wire. The connectors normally used are referred to as 'line taps' which are of different types and sizes but all are designed to firmly clamp the supply cable onto the element tail with a screw or bolt connection. Connector blocks having barrel connectors with two screws are also widely used. Some kilns e.g. Olympic and Skutt use special crimp connectors to attach the supply cable to the element tail. These work well but they are rather more difficult for DIY replacement because they require the use of special crimping pliers. Generally speaking, the larger the size of the metal connecting device, the better will be the electrical connection and the less the risk of arcing

and burning out. This may be due in part to the larger surface area of the connector acting as a heat sink to help dissipate the heat from the hot element tail.

With very small kilns the elements may all be in series but with larger kilns the elements are usually arranged in 'banks' of several elements, each bank being wired in parallel but each element within the bank being wired in series.

Figure 6.4 Two element groups wired in parallel banks, the elements within each bank being wired in series

With three phase kilns it is common for each phase to supply a separate bank of three or more elements.

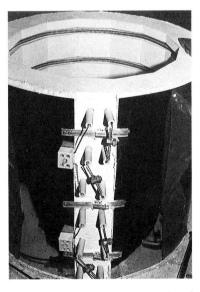

Top-loading kiln construction: view showing the porcelain lead-in insulation tubes, line taps and element connector blocks used to secure the element tails

Element connector block and line taps

The element tails pass through the bricks into the connection chamber. Porcelain insulator tubes are used to avoid grounding the element tails with any metal parts of the switchbox. A common problem is that furnace gases can pass down these insulator tubes (especially the topmost ones) and attack the line tap connection if this is close to the end of the tube – as it often is. For this reason the tail is sometimes bent down and the connection to the element below is made at a lower point than the insulation tube so that it is out of the way of intruding gases.

Connection Cables

Three different cable types are commonly used in wiring kilns dependent upon ambient temperature. The internal wiring of wall-mounted control boxes, which are well away from the heat of the kiln, can be done in PVC-covered wiring cable. Where switchboxes are attached to kilns (as in most top loaders) or in the rear connection chamber of front-loading kilns, wiring should be done using cable designed to withstand higher temperatures. Basically there are two different types of heat resistant cable. A material called tri-rated cable is commonly used. This will withstand temperatures up to about 115°C and has a specially heat-resistant plastic coating. Even so, where such cable is used to make the connections to the elements then, dependent upon the size of the cable and type and size of the line tap, the temperature at the connection point may cause the cable covering to melt or char. For these situations, a special cable covered with a glass fibre impregnated mesh or similar is often used. This cable is designed to withstand temperatures in excess of 250°C, but it is comparatively

expensive and for this reason its use is generally limited to the connections made to the elements.

Wire Connections

Most cables are of the stranded wire variety although it is possible to get a solid cable core instead of a stranded one. Stranded cables have the advantage that they deform more readily under the action of a fixing screw and thus may give a better electrical contact. However, care has to be taken when making really firm connections – as is necessary in a kiln – to ensure that the securing screw on a terminal in, say, a contactor, or at a line tap, does not break the wire strands. To help avoid this, most contactors and some line taps have a small plate which is forced down by the fixing screw to make the actual connection with the cable. Some people 'tin' or solder the wire strands. Others sometimes use a barrel tube connector to slip over the stranded cable to prevent excessive splaying of the strands.

Particular care has to be taken when cutting back the cable insulation to avoid accidentally cutting through any of the strands. This effectively reduces the cable size at that point and if sufficient cable strands are cut through it may overheat and burn out at this point.

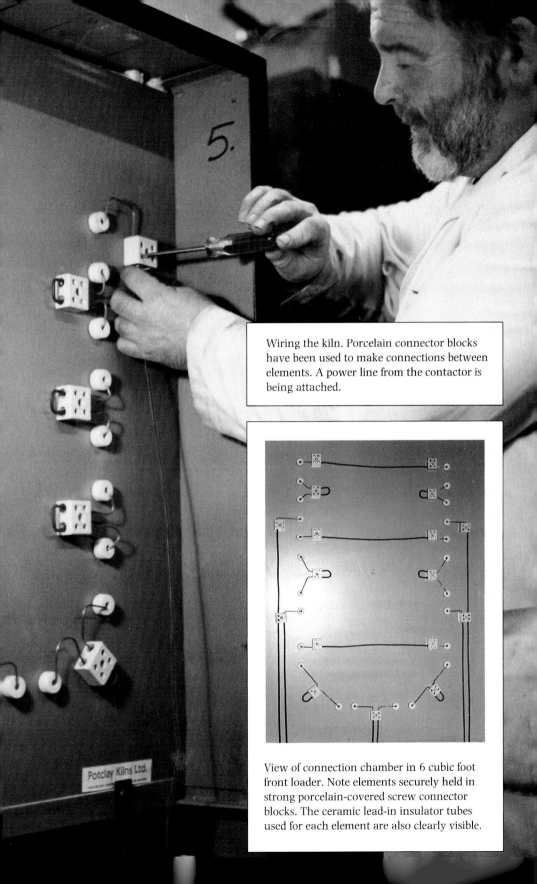

5.

Wiring the kiln. Porcelain connector blocks have been used to make connections between elements. A power line from the contactor is being attached.

View of connection chamber in 6 cubic foot front loader. Note elements securely held in strong porcelain-covered screw connector blocks. The ceramic lead-in insulator tubes used for each element are also clearly visible.

Potclay Kilns Ltd.

Wiring the Kiln to the Electricity Supply

Installing to the Power Supply

Note: Incorrect wiring can be very dangerous. Therefore, the electrical hook-up of a kiln to the power supply must always be done by a competent person. It is especially important that the cable and the fuse be of the correct rating for the job and that all connections are properly made.

The supply cable from the distribution board to the kiln should first be taken to a wall-mounted isolator or switch fuse unit prominently positioned near to the kiln where it can easily be reached. A separate cable from the kiln is then taken to the isolator or switch fuse unit. This cable should preferably be in a flexible conduit and it should be just sufficiently long to allow the kiln to be moved forward if necessary for servicing. It should not be allowed to touch any other part of the kiln when connected. Where it is connected to the kiln, the cable should be firmly held in a gland and the individual wires must not be too long when connected to the power input terminals as slack wire may contact hot elements wire connections in some kilns. After installation, check that there is good earth continuity.

Colour coding

European colour coding of wires demands that brown be used for the live wire, blue

45 amp switch fuse unit

for the negative and green with yellow band for the earth wire.

In the USA, black is used for the live wire, with red or white as the neutral and green for earth (ground).

Prior to the adoption of European colour coding, the UK used red for the live wire, black for the neutral and green for earth – almost the opposite of the USA colour coding system. Care therefore has to be taken to correctly identify the live wire if modifying the wiring of American kilns in the UK (and vice versa).

In practice, most American kilns utilise Kiln Sitter control systems. These have double pole switches which switch both the line and the neutral wires and therefore are a safeguard against inadvertently switching the neutral wire instead of the correct procedure of always switching the live wire. Nevertheless, care is needed to ensure correct polarity when installing other equipment, temperature controllers etc. on the kiln.

Chapter Seven
Elements

A conductor is a substance which allows electric current to flow through it with ease. Metals are the best conductors but even they are not perfect conductors and thus there is some resistance to the flow of electrons which comprises the current flowing through the conductor. The energy needed to overcome this resistance is converted to heat and causes a rise in temperature of the conductor. If a conductor is to be used for heating purposes, it needs to be made of a material which has a sufficiently high resistance and a sufficiently high melting temperature to enable it to heat to high temperatures. And so it is with kiln elements.

There are several different types of element wire which can be fitted to kilns but the most popular ones are those made of Kanthal wire of which there are several grades. Other element materials include Nichrome, Fecralloy and silicon carbide. Let us now look at each of these element types in turn.

Nichrome Elements

Nickel-chromium (80 Ni, 20 Cr) is the oldest resistance heating alloy, the first patent being issued in 1905. Later, other formulations were developed which contained iron as a part replacement for some of the nickel.

Nichrome elements are commonly used in kilns which are not required to operate at temperatures above about 1100°C. Above this temperature the element life very rapidly diminishes.

Consequently, nichrome elements tend to be fitted in low-temperature kilns used for biscuit, low-temperature earthenware or decoration firings and in kilns for lost wax processing, glass slumping etc.

Nichrome wire is comparatively cheap and is the wire also used for domestic electric fires. Incidentally, a free flow of air around electric-fire elements helps to keep the wire element temperature within reasonable limits. For this reason one cannot use the wire from a domestic fire in a kiln situation since within the enclosed kiln such wire would rapidly burn away.

'Hairpin' element

Kanthal Elements

Kanthal wire is an alloy of iron, aluminium and chromium. It was first introduced in the early 1930s and enabled a substantial increase in the maximum temperature of metallic heating elements. There are various grades of Kanthal wire ranging from Alkrothal for low-temperature work, Kanthal D for temperatures up to about 1200°C, Kanthal A-1 for temperatures up to 1300°C and Kanthal AF, also for temperatures up to 1300°C. There is also a Super Kanthal grade for temperatures up to 1500°C. Until recently, Kanthal A-1 was easily the most popular wire for use in electric kilns but increasingly, Kanthal

AF is coming into use on account of its somewhat better form stability, its better hot strength at high temperatures and its superior oxidation resistance.*

The useful life of Kanthal A-1 and Kanthal AF is between two and four times longer than that of NiCr alloys depending on the working temperature. It will be seen from Figure 7.2 for example, that at a temperature of 1100°C the Kanthal wire should last about 3000 hours compared to 1200 hours for Nichrome and at 1150°C, about 1700 hours against 500 for Nichrome.

An important feature of Kanthal wire is that after firing, the wire builds up a layer of aluminium oxide on its surface which protects the wire from attack by harmful furnace gases. It takes two or three firings for this protective layer to form and for this reason the initial firings of a new kiln or one fitted with new elements should be test or biscuit firings rather than glaze ones due to the much more corrosive nature of the gases liberated in glaze firings. Also, exposure to reducing atmosphere will remove the protective coating and the elements will then rapidly deteriorate unless the coating is restored by an oxidising fire. This is why reduction firings in an electric kiln should always be followed by at least one 'clean' oxidising fire (see Chapter 16). **Even so, it must be repeated that reduction firings significantly reduce element life.**

At the time of writing (1993), a British company, Resistalloy, also now produces a similar Fecralloy wire to AF which is coming into significant use after extensive field testing. In most cases, the two wires are interchangeable but there are small differences in the resistivity of each type when at high temperature which sometimes requires a new element calculation to be carried out to obtain matching performance. However, generally, the Fecralloy wire appears to be similar to AF in its characteristics and service life.

A disadvantage with Kanthal is that it becomes quite soft at high temperatures but increasingly brittle after repeated firings when cold. If a kiln is allowed to exceed its maximum designed temperature, the element temperature (which is restrained by the cooler temperature of the kiln) will rise and the element coils may fall over or collapse – thus demonstrating this softness. Similarly, attempts to move or reshape aged elements when they are cold will likely cause them to break. Heating the elements does however make them more flexible and in this way, quite brittle elements can be reshaped to a certain degree.

The need to slightly reshape wire elements sometimes occurs with both NiCr and Kanthal types. This is because all elements very slightly grow in length with use and tend to bulge out of their element channels. This tendency, incidentally, is much accentuated in top loaders by a sudden chilling of elements as happens when the lid is 'cracked open' too soon. Cold air chills and fixes the element surface facing into the kiln and the hot element surface behind it then shrinks towards it. Consequently, the elements tend to climb out of their channels. With front loaders the element coils tend to move towards the door if this is being opened too early and one sometimes sees the apparently baffling phenomenon of elements which have had a redistribution of their coils, most of which are now bunched near the door and comparatively few towards the rear of the kiln.

The fact that elements grow in size and also are influenced by chilling is a particular problem where elements have to pass around an angle such as in six- or eight-sided top loaders, or where they have to turn through 90 degrees as with the junction of two walls in square-section types. Element pins are often used in these situations to ensure the elements are restricted in movement. These pins are pieces of element wire about 2 in. (51 mm) or 3 in. (76 mm) long which are inserted between the coils and pushed into the brickwork like skewers to hold the element in position. Element pins are particularly useful too where there are long element runs. An example of this is with the Olympic 30 cu. ft. rectangular section top loader which has the elements securely pinned every 8 in. (20 cm) or so along its length.

A further problem with all elements is that their electrical resistance changes with temperature. Kanthal A-1 for example increases its resistance by about 3 per cent at 900°C and 4 per cent at 1300°C. This may need to be allowed for when calculating element data.

Silicon Carbide Elements

Often referred to by their 'Glowbar', 'Crusilite' and 'Hot Rod' trade names, silicon carbide elements are normally used only for very high temperature work in kilns firing up to 1500°C. They are made in the form of rods which are dark grey or black in colour. Their service life is superior to both Kanthal and Nichrome types but since their cost is a factor of several times higher than both they are not a cost effective alternative for normal usage.

The electrical resistance of silicon carbide elements changes so significantly with repeated firings that voltage regulators have to be fitted which further increases the cost. An added problem is that expansion during firing gives rise to difficulties in fixing the elements securely into position.

A major advantage of silicon carbide however is that it is unaffected by reduction atmosphere. In the early 1970s, Wengers Ltd made a kiln for the studio ceramics market with silicon carbide elements and a small gas burner to create a reduction atmosphere. It had limited success due to its inevitably high price and the later development of competitively-priced gas kilns for those who needed to reduction fire. At the moment silicon carbide remains an interesting element material which is confined to very high temperature applications.

Electrical Resistance and Ohm's Law

Electrical resistance increases with length and it increases as the cross section becomes smaller. A thin wire will therefore have higher resistance than a thicker one. Similarly, a longer wire of the same thickness will have a higher resistance than a shorter one.

The electrical resistance of a conductor can be measured and expressed in ohms. The current flowing through it can be measured in amps and this will vary proportionally with the voltage applied. If the voltage is doubled, the current is doubled. However, the current varies inversely with the resistance: if the resistance is doubled (and the voltage remains the same), the current flowing will be halved. Simply expressed, the current varies directly with the voltage and inversely with the resistance. This is in accordance with Ohm's Law which is expressed as

$$\frac{E}{I} = R$$

where E is the voltage, I is the current in amps and R is the resistance in ohms.

This can of course be rewritten as

$$I = \frac{E}{R} \quad \text{or} \quad E = I \times R$$

Given a knowledge of two of these factors we can therefore easily calculate the third using Ohm's Law. As an example, suppose that we need to know what length of element wire will allow a current of 13 amps to flow from a 240 volt supply. Applying Ohm's Law:

$$\frac{240}{13} = R. \quad \text{R therefore equals } 18.46 \text{ ohms}$$

The resistance of element wires is stated in the Kanthal handbook for each thickness of wire. If using 16s gauge A1 wire for example, the resistance is quoted as 0.721 ohms per metre. So, if the element wire has a resistance of 0.721 ohms per metre, then dividing 18.46 by 0.721 gives 25.6 metres of element wire.

Wire Size

The wire sizes commonly used for elements vary from BS 12 gauge (about 2.64 mm diameter) to 18 gauge (about 1.2 mm diameter). The thicker the wire, the more expensive the element becomes because the wire has lower electrical resistance and more wire is therefore needed to attain the required element resistance. On the other hand, the larger gauge wires give a longer life. Most studio kilns use wires between 14s and 17s gauge.

A thin element wire reaches a higher surface temperature than a thicker one of the same wattage. Although they both give off the same amount of heat, the thinner wire has smaller mass and the heat has to be radiated from a smaller surface. The difference is very marked if the elements are in free air (as with an electric fire) and is indicated by Figure 7.1

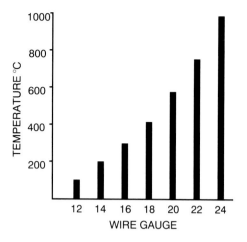

Figure 7.1 Temperatures reached by 1000 watt elements of various gauges in free air

a) KANTHAL A-1   d) NIKROTHAL 80 plus
b) KANTHAL AF   e) NIKROTHAL 60 plus
c) KANTHAL D   f) NIKROTHAL 40 plus

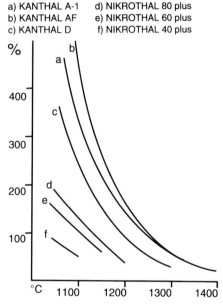

1) At max 1400°c 2550°F only A-1 or AF can be u A-1 will obtain about 10% longer life than AF at 1400°C 2550°F due to its better oxidation propert at temperatures above 1300°C 2310°f.

2) At 1100°C it will be seen that A1 wire has approx 350% better life than at 1200°C and AF about 450% better.

Figure 7.2 Comparative life (KANTHAL A1 at 1200°C 2190°F = 100%)

56

which shows the temperature attained by seven 1000 watt elements of different gauge. In such a situation, a continuous flow of cool air carries away much of the heat generated and has most effect on the thicker wires having the larger surface areas. Inside a kiln it is a different situation since the air temperature progressively approaches the element temperature. Nevertheless, the thinner wires do reach higher temperatures and this is the major reason for their shorter life when compared with elements of thicker wire but of the same wattage.

Kilowatts and Kiln Size

The power of a kiln is determined by its kilowatt rating, one kilowatt being 1000 watts. The kilowatt rating of a kiln is always stated on the data plate and is quoted in the manufacturer's literature. Knowing the kilowatt rating and also the voltage we can calculate the current drawn by the kiln using the formula:

$$\text{Watts} = \text{Volts} \times \text{Amps}$$

the number of kilowatts required to heat a kiln to stoneware is indicated in Figure 7.3. From this it will be seen that small kilns (1–2 ft) need about 3 kW per cu. ft; medium size (4–12 ft) around 1.7 kW per cu. ft. and large kilns about 1.25 kW per cu. ft.

This data of course refers to kilns firing to stoneware but if a kiln is required only for earthenware temperatures then the required kilowatts can be reduced by about 20 per cent.

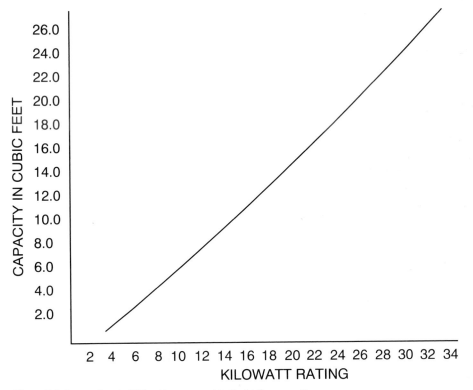

Figure 7.3 Approximate kW rating per cubic foot kiln capacity

Element Layout Calculation

In calculating the element specification for any kiln, a preliminary requirement is to determine how many elements are to be fitted to the kiln and their location. With modern materials and with kilns up to about 30 in. (76.5 cm) internal width and/or less than 10 cu. ft. it is usually sufficient to have elements in the two side walls and the hearth. With larger dimensions, elements may be needed in the rear wall and perhaps also in the door if stoneware temperatures are to be easily reached. The more elements fitted to a kiln, the more efficient it tends to be but there are practical limits as to how many can be fitted into the available brickwork.

As an example, let us suppose we need to calculate an element specification for a kiln which is to operate from a 240 volt supply and has a firing chamber 18 in. wide × 22 in. deep × 27 in. high (44.6 × 56 × 68.7 cm). Multiplying these dimensions together calculates the capacity to be 10,692 cu. in. There are 1728 cu. in. per cu. ft. so dividing 10,692 by 1728 converts this to 6.19 cu. ft. Referring to Figure 7.3, we can see that we need about 10 kilowatts to enable the kiln to reach stoneware.

The internal height of the kiln is 27 in. (68.7 cm). Since the kiln bricks are $4\frac{1}{2}$ in. (11.5 cm) high, this represents six bricks in height. We can put two grooves in each brick to hold a single 'hairpin' element (see Figure 7.4) and we can therefore fit six elements in each of the two side walls. A further three elements will easily fit into the base making a total of 15 elements.

With very small kilns all the elements can be wired together in series but wherever possible it is best to divide the elements into 'banks', each having an independent power supply. We can therefore split the elements into two or three or more banks which will be wired in parallel, the elements in each group or bank being wired in series. Splitting into three parallel circuits (or multiples of three for large kilns) is particularly useful because it facilitates attachment to a three phase supply.

Let us therefore divide our 10 kW kiln into three element banks each containing five elements. With this arrangement, each bank, rated at 3.33 kW, will be wired in parallel, each zone containing five elements wired in series. A separate line supply from the contactor will therefore feed the top five elements in the

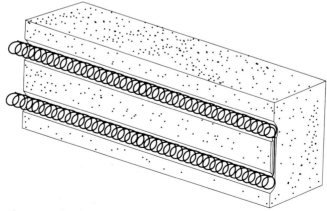

Figure 7.4 Hairpin element in brick

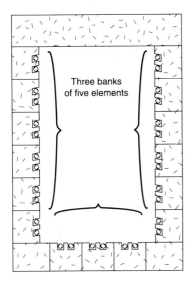

FRONT VIEW SECTION

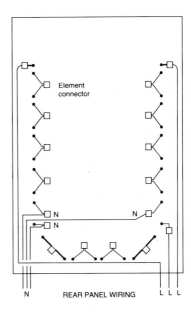

N   REAR PANEL WIRING   L L L

Figure 7.5 Element layouts

left-hand wall, a further separate line would feed the top five elements in the right-hand wall and the third line would feed the bottom three in the hearth plus the bottom element in each of the two side walls (see Figure 7.5).

The total current drawn by the kiln can be calculated by the formula:

$$\text{Watts} = \text{Volts} \times \text{Amps}.$$

Amps therefore equals

$$\frac{\text{Watts}}{\text{Volts}} \text{ i.e. } \frac{10,000}{240} = 41.67 \text{ amps}$$

We will therefore need to protect the kiln via a 45 amp fuse in the wall fuse box.

In fact, the actual current drawn by the kiln is invariably found to be less than that calculated for cold wire because of the change in resistance of the elements at high temperature. Kanthal A1 has four per cent higher and AF wire has six per cent higher resistance at 1300° and the current drawn therefore reduces by these amounts as the kiln heats up.

Element Calculation

Since each of the three elements circuits is rated at 3.33 kW the current drawn by each circuit can be calculated as previously i.e.

$$\text{Amps} = \frac{\text{Watts}}{\text{Volts}} \qquad \text{Amps} = \frac{3333}{240} = 13.9$$

This is confirmed and cross-checked by dividing the total current (41.67 amps) by three to arrive at the same figure of 13.9 amps. Having determined the current drawn by each element bank, the next stage is to calculate the resistance of the element bank. Applying Ohm's Law:

$$\frac{E}{I} = R \qquad \frac{240 \text{ volts}}{13.9 \text{ amps}} = 17.3 \text{ ohms}$$

So, we need a total element resistance of 17.3 ohms in a bank of five elements wired in series. Each element will therefore have a resistance of one-fifth of the total i.e. 3.46 ohms.

Having determined the required element resistance the next step is to

59

decide what wire and wire size to use. Let us assume we wish to use Kanthal AF wire. The optimum wire size demands a consideration of the watts loading of the element but knowing that 14s to 16s gauge is the popular range let us opt for 14s gauge wire which from the Kanthal data sheet is known to have a resistance of 0.442 ohms per metre length. Dividing the required element resistance of 3.46 ohms by 0.442 gives a required length of 7.83 m of Kanthal AF per element.

Other Factors

There are other considerations which should be taken into account in element calculation and which influence the life of an element. These include the watts loading (which is the wattage of an element compared to its surface area), the optimum distance between the individual spirals of an element coil, and also the fact that the resistance of an element changes with temperature. The calculation method given earlier is therefore an over-simplification since the precise, correct calculation is a relatively complex one. Nevertheless, many elements are calculated exactly as the example given and prove to be very satisfactory in both performance and element life.

A further consideration is that if the elements are of identical wattage, it is likely that there will be some temperature variation between top and bottom dependent on firing temperature. At low temperatures – for example a decorating fire to 750°C – the top of the kiln may get much hotter than the bottom (due to heat convection). At high temperature with the same kiln, the middle zone may be a little higher in temperature than the top and bottom zones. This is due to the

middle zone not having the adjacent influence of a cold lid or roof or a relatively cool hearth. If the kiln is needed to fire across a range of temperatures, it is generally best to control any temperature variation by separately controlling the power supply to each zone, usually achieved by fitting an energy regulator to each. The problem of the middle zone always being a little hotter can alternatively be overcome by either slightly reducing the wattage of the middle zone elements or by increasing the spacing between the elements in the middle zone. Some kiln manufacturers leave a full element gap.

Shaping the Elements

Elements are usually shaped into coils by winding the wire onto a rod or mandrell mounted on a motor driven lathe. About 9 in. (23 cm) or so is left as a 'tail' which is attached to the mandrell. As the mandrell is slowly rotated, the wire is fed on to the mandrell, each turn being butted up against the previous coil. Winding is stopped when 9 in. (23 cm) or so remains.

Element closely coiled; same element stretched; same element formed into a hairpin.

The close coiled wire is removed from the mandrell and then stretched to the desired length which, if it is to be a hairpin element, is dictated by double the length of the element groove (to allow for the 'return' length of the hairpin). Finally, the element coil is unwound at the appropriate point (usually halfway along its length) to give a short straight section where the element is to transfer from one groove to the one adjacent to it.

The diameter of the mandrell and thus the diameter of the coil is an important consideration. If the wire gauge is fairly thick, there will likely be a lot of wire used in making an element and a larger diameter mandrell will probably be needed to use up all the wire without having the individual coils too close to each other. Ideally, the diameter of the wire coils should be about five or six times the thickness of the wire but in practice many kiln manufacturers exceed this ratio to a certain degree. A further consideration is that the stretched length of the element coils should be about $1\frac{1}{2}$ to 2 times the close wound length to produce a satisfactory coil pitch spacing.

Installing the Elements

Elements in front-loading kilns should be slightly shorter than the length they are to occupy. The element tails are firstly pushed through element entry holes and porcelain lead-in tubes located through the rear wall and then secured with line taps or other connectors in the connection chamber. The element can be pulled slightly to locate it into the element grooves. Care should be taken not to permanently stretch the element: it must be under tension when installed into the element grooves to help prevent subsequent bulging into the firing chamber.

With round top loaders the situation is reversed. Here the element needs to be a little longer than the groove it is to occupy. The sequence of installation is that an element tail is inserted through its hole leading to the connection box, and secured in position. The element is then fed into its groove until it is in position and finally the remaining element tail is fed into the connection chamber and secured. Because the element coil length is a little longer than the groove it is to occupy, it is usually necessary then to slightly reposition the element by working along it until the bulge (arising from the fact it is a little longer than the groove) is fully taken up. This results in the element sitting well back in its groove and under slight compression in comparison to the slight tension of an element in a front loader.

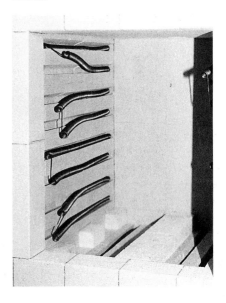

Elements secured to connectors ready for clipping into position in element channels

Chapter Eight
Pyroscopes and Firing Control

Some way of controlling the firing of a kiln is essential to obtain consistently good ceramic ware. Before the intensive study of pyrometric practice, the sense organs were the only means of determining temperatures and kiln firemen estimated the temperature of a kiln by reference to the degree and colour of the glow inside it. The determination of temperature by sight and feel, however, can only be an approximation and it is quite inadequate for modern industrial practices and the requirements of the craft potter.

Pyroscopes and Pyrometers

There are basically two methods of controlling a kiln firing: by the use of pyroscopes and by the use of pyrometers. Pyroscopes are devices which shrink or deform in proportion to the amount of heat they receive and although this can be related to the temperature to which they have been subjected it is not a direct measurement of temperature. For the accurate measurement of temperature we need a pyrometer. Pyroscopes and pyrometers are however often used in conjunction because they measure two different functions i.e. pyroscopes measure heat work, pyrometers measure temperature.

Pyroscopes are indicators made of ceramic mixtures based on silicates. The chemical nature of silicate mixtures is such that they do not have definite melting points but they have a temperature range in which part of the mixture is melted and the remainder is solid. In this temperature range the process of glass formation (vitrification) takes place. When a sufficient degree of vitrification occurs, the pyroscope gives a visible signal either by deforming or shrinking (dependent upon type). There are, however, two ways of attaining this result. The first is to quickly heat the pyroscope to a temperature high enough to produce this effect. The second is to heat it to a lower temperature but to hold this temperature for a longer time.

Since pyroscopes tend to be of similar composition to ceramic clay bodies, they offer a very good means of controlling the finishing point of a kiln firing. Ceramic ware is correctly fired when the correct degree of vitrification has taken place – as are pyroscopes. If a kiln firing is done slowly this optimum firing point will be reached at a lower temperature than when the firing is done very quickly. Thus the reliance on pyrometers alone to determine the finishing point of a kiln firing can be a little misleading.

There are various types of pyroscopes. The most popular type is the pyrometric cone but bars and Bullers rings are also widely used.

Pyrometric Cones

These offer the most important and useful way of controlling or monitoring kiln firings.

Cones are generally offered in two sizes: 'standard' or 'large' cones which are $2\frac{1}{2}$ in. (63 mm) tall and 'small' cones which are 1 in. (26 mm) tall. The cones themselves are of a three-sided conical shape. They are made of carefully controlled mixtures of ceramic materials, the mixtures being designed to give a graduated scale of fusing temperatures at approximately 20°C intervals.

The cones which melt at the lower temperatures contain a higher proportion of fluxes than those melting at the higher temperatures. The melting or fusing temperature of each cone is denoted by a number which is stamped into one side and by reference to the pyrometric cone chart, one can obtain an approximate melting point for each cone number. It is, however, a common misconception that pyrometric cones will always melt at the temperature indicated on this chart. They will only do so if they are fired at the precise rate specified.

If they are fired more rapidly than the specified rate then they will not collapse until a temperature is reached which may be considerably above that indicated by the number stamped on them. Similarly, if the cones are fired too slowly then they will probably collapse at a temperature earlier than that indicated by the cone number. In this way pyrometric cones give an indication of the amount of heat work applied to the ware and not merely the temperature to which the ware is subjected. Consequently, it is common for the temperature indicated by the collapse of a cone to differ by 20°C or 30°C or more from the actual temperature in the kiln. Nevertheless, it is the cone reading which one should rely on.

It should be noted that other factors can influence the temperature at which pyrometric cones collapse. If they are used in a strongly reducing atmosphere then it is possible for a chemical reaction to take place which results in a hard refractory skin being formed on the outside of the cone. The cone may then remain upright well beyond the temperature at which the cone should have collapsed. Sulphur gases can also attack pyrometric cones resulting in bloating and a grey discoloration which, again, tends to distort the collapsing temperature.

One of the most important considerations is the way in which the cones are mounted. This is generally done by inserting the base of the cones either into special cone holders or into a pad of plastic clay, but regardless of the type of mounting it is important that all the cones be embedded to the same depth and that the base surface of the cone is horizontal. It is necessary for the cones to be placed at an angle to the vertical and to ensure this the cones are built with their vertical axes being at an angle to the cone base. The required inclination is therefore automatically brought about when the cone is mounted with its base in the horizontal plane.

Orton cones after and before firing

It is customary to use a series of three cones for each firing. One cone, indicating a temperature about 20°C below the temperature to which the ware is to be fired, one cone indicating the required temperature, and one cone indicating some 20°C above the required one. In this way the collapse of the lower cone serves as a warning that the temperature is rising to the point where the second cone will collapse (at which time the kiln should of course be switched off). The third cone serves as a guard – as an indication that ware has not been overfired. An alternative layout sometimes used by the craft potter is to dispense with the 'guard' cone and to use an extra warning cone which will collapse at a temperature some 40°C below the required temperature of the fire.

It is normal to place the cones from left to right in order of increasing fusion points so that the cone on the extreme right will be the last to go down. The correct firing of any cone is indicated when the cone bends over so that its tip

touches the base on which the cone is mounted. This is referred to as the 'end-point' of the cone. If the temperature continues to increase then the cone will of course, collapse still further and eventually melt completely.

Orton Cone Chart

| ORTON CONE No. | Approx. bending temp. °C (Temp. equivalent) | | |
| | Heating rate °C per hour | | |
	60°C	100°C	150°C
018	712	722	732
017	736	748	761
016	769	782	794
015	788	802	816
014	807	822	836
013	837	848	859
012	858	869	880
011	873	883	892
09	917	922	928
08	942	948	954
07	973	979	985
06	995	1002	1011
05	1030	1038	1046
04	1060	1065	1070
03	1086	1093	1101
02	1101	1110	1120
01	1117	1127	1137
1	1136	1147	1154
2	1142	1152	1162
3	1152	1160	1168
4	1160	1181	1170
5*	1184	1194	1205
6*	1220	1230	1241
7*	1237	1246	1255
8*	1247	1259	1270
9	1260	1270	1280
10	1282	1293	1303
11	1293	1303	1312

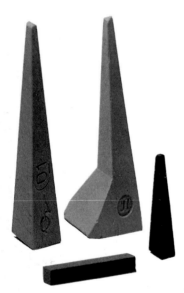

Orton large cone, self-supporting cone, small cone and minibar

There are three types of pyrometric cone in use: Staffordshire or Al cones manufactured in the UK; Orton cones manufactured in the USA and Seger cones manufactured in Germany. Since Seger were the first in the field the name has become a generic term but this can be misleading for it is a fact that if theoretically the same Al, Orton and Seger cones are fired together, they do not collapse exactly together. Thus, one cannot change from one cone type to another without prior evaluation by simple comparison tests. Orton cones, incidentally, are the ones most widely used and these tend to be about 1 to $1\frac{1}{2}$ cones softer than Seger.

Bullers Rings

Bullers rings are widely used in the industry and take the form of a flat ring some 3 in. (76 mm) in diameter and about $\frac{1}{4}$ in. (6 mm) thick. They have a hole in the middle so that when they are stood upright on special holders, they can be hooked out of the kiln using special draw rods inserted through ports in the side of the kiln.

After firing, the rings will have contracted and the degree of contraction can be measured by placing the ring into a Bullers ring gauge. The gauge is marked with a scale which is calibrated from zero (zero being the indicated reading of an unfired Bullers ring). The ring number gives a very approximate indication of temperature by applying the formula: 960 plus seven times the Bullers ring number. However, this unwieldy equation is purely academic; the function of the Bullers ring, as with a cone, is to give an indication of the heat work carried out.

Bullers rings are not commonly used by studio potters because of the expense of the gauge and the amount of space taken up by the ring during firing. They are however widely used by the larger industrial concerns because of their uniform rate of contraction over a wide range of temperature. Even so, there are five different rings for different temperature ranges.

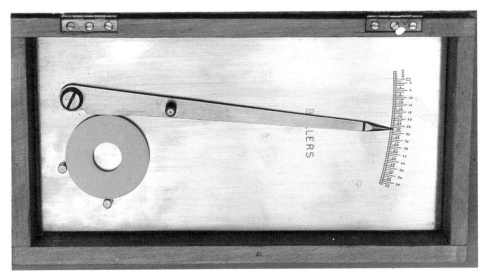

Bullers Ring in gauge (*Taylor, Tunnicliffe Ltd.*)

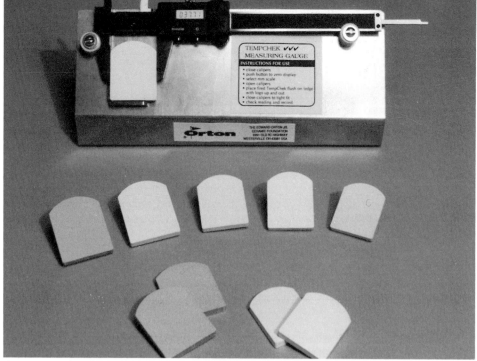

Orton TempCheck system

Orton TempChek

Introduced by Orton in 1993, this is an alternative system which very accurately measures the fired shrinkage of small ceramic plaques to determine heat work.

Bell and Holdcroft Bars

These are an alternative form of pyroscope which take the form of bars of ceramic material of about $\frac{1}{4}$ in. (6 mm) square cross section and about 3 in. (76 mm) in length. They are stamped with a number from 1 to 40 which can be related to a chart graduated from 600°C to 1550°C.

Bell minibars are manufactured in the USA and Holdcroft bars in the UK. Both types are placed horizontally onto supports so that only the ends of the bars are supported. The ceramic mixtures of which they are made cause a progressive softening as they approach the

approximate firing temperatures indicated in reference charts. At the appropriate point the bars bend or collapse in the middle thus giving a visible signal.

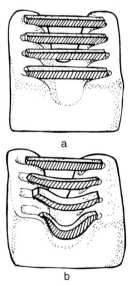

Figure 8.1 Holdcraft bars (a) before using (b) after using

Chapter Nine
Thermocouples and Thermoelectricity

The basic form of pyrometer is a simple temperature-indicating device consisting of a thermocouple and a galvanometer or millivolt meter calibrated to read temperature. In addition, there are a wide range of indicators and temperature controllers of varying degrees of sophistication but whatever the instrument, all function by interpreting the signal received from a thermocouple. The thermocouple is therefore the 'working end' of a pyrometer. It is normally inserted through the wall or roof of a kiln so that the tip projects into the firing chamber and, when heated, it generates a voltage which is measured by the instrument fixed outside the kiln.

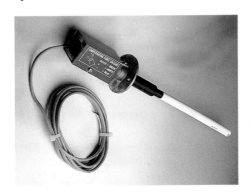

Thermocouple with compensating cable
(*Industrial Pyrometer Company*)

The thermocouple is thus an extremely important part of the system and before going on to discuss the different types of temperature indicators and controllers, we should perhaps begin by looking at what thermocouples are and the way in which they function.

Thermocouples

If two different metals are drawn into wires and they are joined together at one end, a small electric current is generated when the joint of the two wires is heated. The greater the amount of heat applied to the junction, the greater will be the voltage generated in the wires. By measuring the voltage one can, therefore, obtain an indication of the amount of heat being applied to the junction of the wires. If this junction is plunged into, say, boiling water the voltage indicated on the instrument can be marked with the temperature 100°C since this is the boiling point of water. Similarly, if the end of the thermocouple is plunged into boiling sulphur, the reading on the instrument can be calibrated for 444°C. Various other reference temperatures can be used and in this way we can calibrate the instrument to read degrees of temperature as well as voltage. Thus we will have produced a thermoelectric pyrometer and we can see that this is made up of a thermocouple and galvanometer or millivolt meter with interconnecting cables.

The voltage generated by a thermocouple is very small (being measured in millivolts) and is due to two completely different effects known as the Thomson and Peltier effects respectively.

In 1834 Peltier discovered that when two different metals are joined together, a difference in voltage exists between them and that this varies with the temperature of the junction. In 1854 Thomson discovered that when a length of metallic wire is heated at one end a difference in voltage between the ends is created. Sometimes the heated end is at a higher voltage than the other but sometimes the reverse is true.

When selecting wires from which to make thermocouples, the manufacturers must ensure that the Peltier and Thomson effects complement one another. They must, therefore choose two wires whose Thomson effects are in opposite directions and vary uniformly with temperature. They must also ensure that the voltage generated by the Peltier effect is such that the wire carrying the negative Thomson voltage must be the positive element as far as the Peltier voltage is concerned. The voltage created by the two different effects will then support one another and will tend to vary uniformly with temperature provided that the cold end of the thermocouple is held at a known and constant temperature.

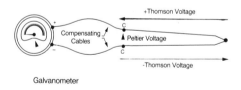

Galvanometer

Figure 9.1 Simplified diagram of thermoelectric pyrometer

The cold end of the thermocouple is generally referred to as the 'cold junction', the end of the thermocouple projecting into the firing chamber being referred to as the 'hot junction'.

It should always be remembered that the voltage generated by the thermocouple is dependent upon the difference in temperature between the hot and cold junctions and to register temperature accurately it is very important for the cold junction to be kept always at the same known temperature. The reason for this is that the wires which connect the cold junction of the thermocouple to the instrument (these wires are known as compensating cables) will themselves generate a small voltage between the cold junction of the thermocouple and the instrument. In this case the instrument serves to unite the ends of the compensating cables. The Peltier effect of the compensating cables will vary if the temperature of this junction of the cables also varies. Providing that we keep the cold junction at the thermocouple and the instrument at a constant temperature, the small Peltier voltage generated by the compensating cables via the instrument can be corrected by calibrating the latter.

If heat is applied to the thermocouple or compensating wires at some point along their length, the voltages created by this additional source of heat will tend to cancel themselves out, providing that the respective temperatures of the hot and cold junctions are not affected.

It should be noted that there are several different types of thermocouples and the amount of voltage generated at any particular temperature differs with each type. For this reason temperature indicators and controllers have to be calibrated for a particular thermocouple type and cannot be used with others.

The metals from which the thermocouple wires are made differ with different thermocouple types. Some of the more commonly used thermocouples are as follows:

	Normal range °C	Compensating cable insulation colours	
		British (BS1843) Outer, Inner + Inner −	American Outer, Inner + Inner −
Type K: *Chromel–alumel* Has a positive wire of nickel-chromium alloy and a nickel-aluminium negative wire.	0–1100	See type V below	
Type V: *Copper–copper/nickel* (Constantan) Used as compensating cable for type K thermocouples but only where the interconnection temperature is in the range 0°C–80°C		Red White Blue or Red Brown Blue	Yellow Yellow Red
Type R: *Platinum/13% rhodium – platinum* An alloy of platinum with rhodium for the + wire and pure platinum for the −. Used mainly in UK.	0–1600	See type U below	
Type S: *Platinum/10% rhodium – platinum* Alloy of platinum with rhodium for the + wire and pure platinum for the −. Used mainly in the USA and Europe	0–1550	See type U below	
Type U: *Copper–copper/low value nickel* Used as compensating cable only for type R and S thermocouples but only where interconnection temperature is in the range 0–50°C.		Green White Blue Orange Orange White (European Standard from 1997)	Green Black Red

Notes

The type R is used in the UK in preference to type S for historical reasons. It has high resistance to oxidation and corrosion but is easily contaminated and normally requires protection.

The type S is normally used in the USA and Europe except the UK.

Colour codings for German, French and Japanese thermocouples are different to above.

There are various other thermocouple types but types K, R and S are the types generally used in ceramics.

Thermocouple Construction

The two thermocouple wires are welded at their tip and then passed through porcelain insulators to separate them, the wires then being fitted into a connector block at the 'head' of the thermocouple. It is usual in the UK (less so in the USA) to fit a protective porcelain sheath over the thermocouple wires to help prevent damage by hot gases and also to help avoid physical damage to the welded tip.

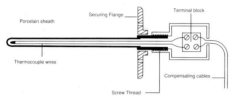

Figure 9.2 Thermocouple: typical cross section

The compensating cable wires are connected to the connector block at the head of the thermocouple ensuring clean, tight connections and the correct polarity. Frequently, the negative terminal is marked with a blue spot to facilitate this.

The head of the thermocouple is generally in the form of a box with a removable cover to enable access to the connector block. If the head tends to become overheated due to incorrect installation or whatever, it often helps to remove the cover to ventilate and help cool what in essence becomes a miniature oven.

Some Points About Installation

It is preferable to mount the thermocouple through the wall of a kiln rather than through the roof. The reason for this is that if the thermocouple is not a reasonably close fit into the hole drilled through to take it, hot gases from the kiln

more easily push their way upwards resulting in overheating of the thermocouple head. If the thermocouple head gets above 50°C (common in lid-mounted thermocouples in top loaders) then the head connecting block acts as a thermocouple tip for the compensating cable. The voltage generated partly cancels the thermocouple voltage giving a low reading on the instrument. Errors can be considerable: frequently, 50°C or more out.

It cannot be over-emphasised that the head of the thermocouple must be kept reasonably cool, otherwise the indicated temperature displayed by the measuring instrument will be lower than the correct figure. Indeed, the most common cause of incorrect reading on a pyrometric indicator or controller is due to a problem with the cold junction temperature of the thermocouple and not with the instrument.

Equally, it is important that the thermocouple should not be positioned through the kiln wall in a location which results in the thermocouple tip being very close to an element as this will result in radiant overheating resulting in a too-high temperature indication on the instrument. If there are no elements in the back wall of a front loader, this is generally the best location for the thermocouple. In top loaders – especially those with $2\frac{1}{2}$ in. or 3 in. thick lids – the walls or the spy holes are much better locations than the lid.

The tip of the thermocouple should project about $1\frac{1}{2}$ in. (4 cm) into the firing chamber. More is unnecessary. As previously mentioned, the entry hole should be just wide enough to take the thermocouple sheath. If there is a slack fit, ceramic fibre can be loosely tamped into the gap to provide a better seal.

Chapter Ten
Temperature-Measuring Instruments

Temperature-measuring instruments are of different types, ranging from the simple temperature indicator to sophisticated controllers which enable both firing and cooling to be fully automated.

The choice of the most suitable instrument obviously will depend not only upon the job it has to do but largely also upon personal preference and to a certain degree upon whether the kiln operator can be constantly available or is only available for short periods to attend the kiln. If one has the time to attend to the kiln whenever necessary to change firing speed, soak at the required temperature, switch off, etc., then manual adjustment of energy regulators to control firing speed, use of cones and fitment of a temperature indicator would suffice. Increasingly however, people are taking advantage of the convenience and time saved by using temperature controllers.

Analogue and digital temperature indicators with thermocouple and compensating cable

The cost of a temperature-indicating pyrometer is basically the cost of the instrument plus the cost of the

thermocouple plus the required length of compensating cable. With temperature controllers, one has also to take the cost of a contactor into account if a suitable one is not already fitted to the kiln. Frequently some rewiring of the kiln secondary circuits is also necessary.

Most temperature indicators and controllers are of a delicate nature and the manufacturers recommend that they be serviced at regular intervals if accuracy and reliability are to be maintained. Furthermore, it is always a wise precaution to carry out the first few firings by reliance on pyrometric cones and to use the instrument solely as a reference – just to ensure that it is functioning correctly. Remember, however, that comparisons of cone and pyrometer readings are very approximate and there may be a significant difference between the temperature reading on the pyrometer and that suggested by the cone chart.

Types of Pyrometer

Pyrometers can broadly be divided into two types: those that merely indicate temperature and those which additionally provide a control function. The latter group are called controllers and range from those which provide only a cut-off facility when the kiln reaches preset temperature to types which enable complete control over the firing cycle to be achieved, including future start facility, multiple firing speed options, cooling speed control, and the ability to ring warning bells, control automatic dampers etc. Some examples are listed below which serve only to show the lower and upper ends of the range normally encountered in craft ceramics. In between there are a variety of others with various features and options.

Indicating Pyrometer

The analogue version usually consists of a galvanometer fitted with a temperature scale, a thermocouple housed inside a porcelain sheath, and a suitable compensating cable for connecting the two. In addition to being calibrated for a particular type of thermocouple, the instrument is invariably calibrated for a particular thermocouple resistance and will give incorrect readings if a significantly different one is used. This often happens when instruments are coupled to old thermocouples which tended to have thicker (and therefore lower resistance) thermocouple wires than the gauges now used. It also can happen when using an instrument from one supplier and a thermocouple from another.

After mounting the instrument on the kiln or nearby wall etc., the thermocouple is positioned through the wall of the kiln (see Installation notes on p. 70). The 'shunt' wire is then removed from the instrument terminals and the compensating cables attached, ensuring correct polarity (blue wire is negative). If a lighted match is then applied to the thermocouple tip, the indicator needle should respond in a few seconds. If the needle moves the wrong way then the wire connections have been reversed either at the thermocouple head or, more likely, the connections made to the

instrument, in which case just change them over.

Digital indicating pyrometers are more expensive than the analogue ones. They are not necessarily more accurate but a digital display does make it easier to control a soaking period since the changing numbers indicate much more clearly whether the temperature is going up or down. There are two types, those powered by a small battery and those which are mains operated. The latter type needs a power supply which would normally be taken from the ancillary supply circuits in the kiln and protected by a 3 amp fuse.

Studio 1500 controller gives soak or cut-off option at adjustable preset temperature (*Industrial Pyrometer Company*)

Limitronic

Known by other trade names such as Thermolimit, Studio 1500 etc., this instrument enables the required firing temperature to be manually preset into the instrument. When this temperature is reached the instrument either cuts off the kiln or maintains the preset temperature dependent upon whether a switch on the instrument is set to its cut-off or 'soak' position. If in the 'soak' position, the temperature will be maintained indefinitely until the switch is moved to the cut-off position.

The cheapest type does not give any indication of temperature – and is therefore often referred to as a 'blind' controller. It is however generally possible to approximate the firing temperature by turning back the preset temperature control until a point is reached which causes the kiln to cut off. The temperature setting on the preset-scale can then be read off and the temperature setting restored to its original value – which immediately causes the kiln to switch on again.

More popular is the type which also indicates temperature. There are both analogue and digitally indicating types.

Limitronic Plus gives soak or cut-off option and digital temperature indication

Firemaster 2 and Cambridge 401

These instruments are similar in that they provide digital indication of temperature, a delay start and two fully adjustable

'ramps', enabling the firing speed to be programmed for one speed up to, say, 300°C (referred to as the 'first set point') and then for a different speed up to the 'second set point' which normally would be the required firing temperature. Additionally, they have a timed soak facility so that at top temperature the kiln can be held at this temperature for an adjustable time period after which the kiln is shut down. They are microprocessor-based with all solid state circuitry.

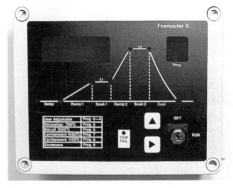

Firemaster 2 temperature controller

The Cambridge instrument enables five different programs to be entered and stored, each consisting of two ramps and a timed soak. Alternatively, the programs can be linked together to provide one program which can have up to 10 ramps and soak periods. In this way it can meet almost any firing cycle requirement.

The Firemaster 2 has five user adjustable programs each consisting of two ramps with an adjustable soak at the end of each and additionally it has five fixed programs designed for ceramics (750°C, 1000°C, 1060°C, 1120°C and 1260°C) which can quickly be set and run. It also has an automatic heat fuse built into the system which triggers at 1325°C. A further feature of the

Firemaster is a maximum firing time facility and this is useful when an element fails on a kiln programmed to fire to high temperature. The kiln may then be incapable of reaching the programmed temperature but remains on at reduced power whilst the controller continually calls for more heat. This can result in the kiln structure becoming heat-soaked as the kiln remains on at elevated temperatures until the problem is discovered and the kiln is shut off. With the Firemaster one can programme a maximum permissible firing time after which the kiln will be shut down automatically.

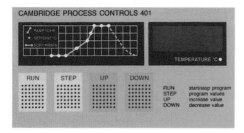

Cambridge 401 controller (*Cambridge Process Controls*)

Both instruments have a simple keypad on the front face which enables the program data to be entered, and a lock facility to prevent unauthorised adjustment of programmed values. They also have a mimic firing curve on the front panel which is fitted with various LEDS which show the program stage and sequence.

By setting the first set point to the maximum required firing temperature and the second set point to a lower figure it is also possible to obtain a controlled cooling rate as well as controlled firing rate.

Controllers such as these give control of the entire firing cycle, giving accurate and repeatable firings.

Differential Temperature Controller

Where it is especially important to obtain a very even temperature from top to bottom in the kiln, a differential temperature control system can be used. This involves having a thermocouple mounted at the top and one at the base of the kiln. In addition, the kiln elements are arranged so that those in the top half of the kiln are controlled by one contactor and those in the bottom are controlled by another. The thermocouples are wired 'back to back' so that the positive of one is coupled to the negative of the other, and vice versa. If both the thermocouples are at the same temperature then their signals will cancel out and there will be no voltage signal fed to the control instrument which effectively is set to 'soak' at 0°C. If a positive signal is received, one thermocouple must be hotter than the other and, if the difference is sufficient, the other control instrument shuts off the contactor feeding current to that zone. In practice, one needs to identify which zone will be the hottest and to use two instruments: one to control and switch the contactor to the hottest zone and one which monitors the temperature of the reference zone.

Differential control systems enable a temperature difference of less than 5°C to be maintained between the two zones.

Other Temperature Controllers

There are a great variety of instruments which have a range of features in between those of the Limitronic and Firemaster types and these may be perfectly adequate for many processes. There are also a number of controllers which are even more sophisticated, enabling even the most complicated firing cycle to be operated.

One problem with most temperature controllers – especially when fitted to kilns which have a relatively high power rating in relation to their capacity – is that of 'overshoot'. When the kiln temperature exceeds the programmed temperature, the controller temporarily cuts off the kiln until the temperature falls to below the programmed level and the controller then switches power back on again. However, the firing speed impetus of the kiln when full on causes the temperature to continue to rise for a short while despite the controller having shut off the power. Consequently there is a 'band width' within which the kiln temperature oscillates when following its programmed temperature rise. Some of the more expensive and sophisticated controllers have the means to compensate for overshoot and undershoot by regulating the power or by reducing the program band width.

Many of the more expensive controllers have all these features and more, including the ability to ring alarm bells, close automatic dampers etc., etc. For these reasons such instruments are popular in the industry but they provide much more than is needed by the craft user and consequently are not cost effective on studio kilns.

Mention must also be made of the microprocessor-based Orton, Bartlett and other controllers which are designed to simulate the performance of Orton cones. These use solid state circuitry and enable you to dial a cone number and select the required heating rate etc. The controller automatically adjusts the firing temperature to conform to the heat work data for the selected cone. As with all other temperature controllers, it is used in conjunction with a thermocouple.

The Kiln Sitter

The Kiln Sitter has been in use for many years but remains a simple but effective way of controlling the end point of a firing without using a thermocouple. It uses the bending action of a small Orton cone or Minibar to operate a switching device to cut off the electrical supply to the kiln. The Kiln Sitter comprises a metal box containing a heavy-duty mechanically-operated switch. Projecting from the box is a robust porcelain tube which passes through the kiln wall into the firing chamber. Two metal cone supports are fitted in the end of the tube and the small cone is placed onto these but also underneath a high-temperature heat-resistant sensing rod which passes through the tube. The other end of the sensing rod terminates in a claw which holds a counterweight in position.

VIEW A

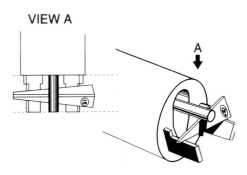

Cone placement

The equipment is set to commence firing by pressing in a self-locating push button to close the switch. When the required firing point has been reached, the cone bends. As the pivoted sensing rod moves downwards to follow the bending action of the cone, the claw end moves upwards thus releasing the counterweight and, in falling, this weight releases with a snap action the heavy-duty switch thus shutting off the kiln.

Kiln Sitter with Limit Timer

The Kiln Sitter is therefore basic in that it provides only a means of cutting off the kiln at the required temperature and does not even have a soak facility as does the Limitronic and other base level temperature controllers. It is possible to manually soak by lifting the counterweight, pressing in the push button to reset the switch, and then resetting the kiln energy regulators to a lower setting but it is a bit 'hit or miss' because one has no visible temperature indication. Nevertheless, its mechanical simplicity makes it a reliable control system with the advantage of being activated by heat work considerations rather than temperature alone.

The Kiln Sitter is also available fitted with a Limit Timer which is activated as soon as the kiln is switched on and should be set for a time period about one hour or so longer than the anticipated firing time. If, for whatever reason, the Kiln Sitter fails to shut off the kiln at the right time, the Limit Timer will do so at the end of its timed run. In conjunction with the Limit Timer, the Kiln Sitter is therefore a simple but effective way of ensuring that the kiln cuts off at the required end point of the firing.

Incidentally, it is of course easily possible to couple a time switch to a temperature controller or in series with the power supply to the contactor holding coil to give the same back-up, safety cut-off system provided by the Limit Timer on a Kiln Sitter. Indeed, some controllers have this 'time-out' facility built in.

Pyrometer Installation: some important points

Pyrometers must not be positioned where they are subject to radiant heat, draughts or dampness and they should be kept as near as possible to normal room temperature. With analogue indicating types it is also very important that they are mounted perfectly level and a spirit level should be used to check this.

A power supply is needed for all temperature controllers and some digital temperature indicators. This would normally be taken from the fused ancillary circuit on the kiln but alternatively an independent supply can be provided but a 3 amp or similar fuse should be fitted in this supply line to protect the instrument. The power output from the controller should be wired either to the energy regulator circuit or to the holding coil of the kiln contactor, or both, depending upon the type of controller. If the controller does not control firing speed then the controller output will always be to the energy regulator circuits. If the controller does control firing speed then the output can be taken directly to the contactor holding coil. In this event any energy regulator fitted to the kiln is rendered superfluous. However, where two or more energy regulators are fitted to a kiln there is some advantage in taking the controller output in parallel to each of the energy regulators. In this way the energy regulators would normally be left full on but could continue to act as proportioning devices to balance up the kiln in the event of uneven firing.

Be careful not to connect mains power supply to an instrument's thermocouple terminals. The results can be quite spectacular with analogue indicating instruments, and quite noisy with digital controllers as the track is blown away from printed circuit boards!

Also check the polarity of the power supply to the instrument if there is any doubt about this. Quite apart from the hazard of electric shock there will likely be serious damage to a controller if neutral is connected to the live instrument terminal and live to neutral.

It is often recommended that capacitors be fitted across the holding coils of contactors if these have not already been fitted by the kiln manufacturers. The breaking action of contactors often generates electronic noise or 'spikes' in the power supply which some temperature controllers are particularly sensitive to, causing a crazy jumping around of the temperature display and incorrect or aborted firings. Fitment of a 0.1 microfarad capacitor to the contactor holding coil can prevent this.

However, this is true only of unscreened controllers. Increasingly, controllers have screening devices fitted into their circuitry and further fitment of a capacitor to the kiln contactor can cause malfunction with some instruments. Therefore do check with the supplier before such fitment.

With analogue temperature indicators it is usually possible to alter the indicating needle position by adjusting a small screw fitted to the front of the instrument. Unfortunately, manufacturers refer to this as the 'zero adjusting screw' and many users consequently use this to adjust the instrument pointer to zero at its rest or start position. This is correct if the kiln interior is indeed at freezing point (0°C) but if the kiln is at room temperature the needle should be adjusted to read room temperature (normally about 20°C).

When analogue instruments are packed for despatch, a connecting wire is fitted between the terminals to which the compensating cable will be attached. This 'shunt' wire damps the movement of the indicator needle, preventing it from violently swinging across the scale when the instrument is jolted in transit etc. and it must be disconnected when the compensating cables are attached.

Chapter Eleven
Kiln Furniture

Batts

In a studio electric kiln, the ware is placed on shelves made from one to four or more kiln batts depending upon the size and shape of which there are several different types.

Kiln batts are available in different thicknesses, the thickest ones – usually $\frac{3}{4}$ in. to 1 in. (2 to $2\frac{1}{2}$ cm) thick – being capable of use for stoneware and porcelain as well as earthenware. Much depends, of course, upon the size of the kiln batt (larger ones needing to be thicker to be able to hold the same load per unit area as smaller ones) and also upon the material from which the batts are made. The best material, but unfortunately by far the most expensive, is silicon carbide or carborundum. Next best – and easily the most popular – are the high-alumina mixtures such as cordierite and sillimanite.

It is possible to make your own shelves from a stiff mixture of equal parts of fireclay and medium – coarse grog which is then packed very densely into a mould with a mallet. When dry, they need to be fired to at least cone 11, using placing sand as a separating agent to prevent sticking. However, they will never be as strong as industrially-manufactured ones of similar thickness.

Testing and Storage of Batts

Kiln batts must be quite dry before being subjected to the normal firing schedule as otherwise they may crack due to escaping steam. Sometimes, fine cracks may appear in a kiln batt due to damage during handling or transit and they may be so fine that they can not be easily seen.

Before batts are put into service they should therefore be carefully but thoroughly dried and sounded. A dry batt can be supported by hand at its centre or suspended between thumb and finger and tapped with a metal object. If it does not ring clearly, a crack may be suspected. Such cracks can often be more easily detected by sprinkling fine alumina powder onto the batt and sharply tapping it in the centre. This causes the powder to move away from any crack in the batt, revealing the crack as a line in the powder.

A dull sound suggests the batt is not dry and further drying is necessary. It is also important to check that kiln batts are perfectly flat as ware placed directly on warped shelves is itself likely to warp – and certain to do so if the ware is porcelain.

Always store batts in a dry place and on edge rather than placed flat.

Kiln Props

There are several different types of kiln prop, the most popular ones being castellated props, tubular props and cast props. Castellated props are basically tubular but have turrets on them which interlock with those on the adjoining castellated prop to form a stable structure. Tubular props are refractory tubes, usually cylindrical, and available in various lengths. Cast props are specially-shaped props which incorporate a foot to spread the load. Spreading the load can be achieved with other props by using 'collars' and 'base supports' which are of greater diameter than the tubular props and are recessed to take them, or by using castellated discs which fit at the top and bottom of a castellated disc column. Such load spreaders are particularly useful where there are two or more batts per shelf and one prop column is supporting two batts. Interlocking extension props are also available which are short, solid props which have a dome at one end and a recess at the other so that they can interlock with each other or with tubular props.

Some potters make their own props from a heavily grogged clay such as Potclays Crank which is rolled into cylinders and fired to high stoneware.

A number of small props will obviously give increased choice of shelf spacings but a series of props one above the other does not give such a stable assembly as one large prop of the same height. Consequently some compromise is necessary when determining a selection of props to give both a stable structure and reasonable ability to vary the height between shelves. Whatever the choice of props, it is essential that they be positioned directly above each other on each shelf so that the weight of the furniture and ware load acts downwards through continuous columns.

With small kilns and especially when firing to earthenware, it is common to use three equidistantly placed props or prop columns rather than four per batt. This saves space and does not allow any rocking. At higher temperatures this may also be possible but much depends upon batt thicknesses, the weight of the ware load they have to carry and how high the temperature. Four prop columns per batt is therefore more common for stoneware and porcelain firings.

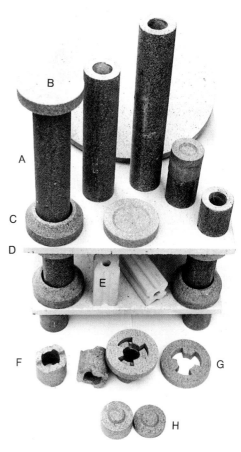

Kiln furniture
A. Tubular props

B. Collar

C. Base support

D. Kiln batts

E. Prop

F. Castellated prop

G. Castellated disc

H. Interlocking extension prop

79

Coating the Shelves: Batt Wash

It is important that the surface of the kiln batts does not contain any irregularities or protruberences that will arrest the firing shrinkage of the wares placed on them, otherwise cracking or distortion of the ware is possible. The best way to assist this shrinkage is to scatter a thin layer of white silica sand on the shelves. Each particle then acts like a ball bearing in assisting the contraction of the ware. This is fine for biscuit firings but during glaze firings a loose, thin layer of silica sand on the shelves can be a nuisance since particles can be dislodged onto glazed ware below, causing rough spots on the fired ware. With glaze firings, a better solution is needed which, more importantly, will also help prevent pots sticking to the kiln shelves. Glazed pots placed onto shelves should not, of course have any glaze whatever on their bases but problems sometimes occur due to inadequate cleaning off or to a spot of glaze having been deposited on the batt surface during loading or firing. The pots can then stick solidly to the shelf and have to be broken away. For these reasons, batt wash is painted onto the top surface of the kiln batts.

Batt washes are generally mixtures of zircon, alumina and China clay (kaolin). The powder mixture is mixed with water and painted onto the batts to completely cover the top surface with a smooth coat. Pots can be placed into position as soon as it is dry and, after firing, the coat should remain as a firm but friable layer. If it is properly applied, any glaze particle on a pot base should result in the batt wash sticking to the pot at that point and being pulled away from the batt when the pot is lifted away. The missing area of batt wash can then be touched in.

After firings, the surface of kiln batts should be checked. Loose particles of wash can be brushed away and more wash painted on if necessary. It is advisable to periodically check batts more thoroughly and to rub down the batt wash with a hand stone. Any particles of glaze adhering to them can be chipped away with a 'sorting' tool or cold chisel and new wash applied. If any kiln batts are cracked they should either be discarded or broken into two pieces for use as half batts etc. If the crack is a minor one it is usually possible to make use of the batt with very little risk of failure, provided that a prop is used to support the batt immediately underneath the cracked area.

If the same kiln is being used for biscuit and glost (glaze) firings, it is best not to use silica sand at all but to rely solely upon the coating of batt wash as the risk of contamination of glazed pots from particles of silica sand is considerable. Incidentally, flint or fine quartz must never be used as a batt wash or powder coating for health reasons.

Batt wash should also be applied to the metal cone supports of a Kiln Sitter and can also be used as a coating to the inside face of the base of a top loading kiln.

Chapter Twelve
Loading the Kiln

Loading or packing a kiln for firing can be an art in itself; with practice you can acquire an eye for compactly packing items into the available space. It can help to firstly divide the items to be fired into roughly similar heights. This can then enable the gapping between the shelves to be adjusted to minimise wasted space.

Placement of Ware

If your kiln has a hot spot, you might need to consider this when you place the ware so that glazes which might be improved by the higher firing can be placed there, or alternatively, very sensitive glazes can be kept clear. Also, because uneven heating causes warping, try to place large bowls in the centre of a kiln shelf where they will receive even heating from all sides. This applies also to tall narrow cylinders: if they are placed on the edge of a shelf they may shrink noticeably more on the side facing the elements, causing them to become banana-shaped.

Generally, the shortest items should be packed on shelves at the bottom of the kiln to help ensure the most stable kiln load. However, if you have very heavy or awkward shaped objects, these would normally be placed at the bottom.

Some potters find it helpful to simulate the space available in the kiln by marking a suitable working surface with a full-scale plan of each kiln shelf. While the kiln is in use, pots can be arranged in their respective firing positions so that when the kiln is ready for repacking, the pots can be quickly transferred to their pre-planned positions in the kiln.

When loading ware for either biscuit or glaze firing, leave a gap of at least 1 in. (26 mm) between the ware and the elements so as to avoid excess shrinkage, vitrification or colour problems on one side of the pot, or warping.

Loading Sequence

With front loaders it is best to load the top shelf first and then to work downwards so that the last ware to be loaded is placed on the bottom shelf. If any bits of grit etc. are dislodged from the shelf during loading, they then fall onto empty shelves below instead of onto ware ready for firing. This of course is one of the main drawbacks with top loaders: one has no alternative to loading the bottom shelves first.

Biscuit Kiln Loading

A most important point is that any clay ware placed into a kiln must be dry. Damp ware is liable to crack or explode (with possible damage to other pots), as a result of steam pressure built up inside it during firing. A useful indicator of whether clay ware is dry is to place it against your cheek. If it feels cold then the ware is damp and must be allowed to dry longer.

Loading a kiln for biscuit firing is simpler than loading one for glaze firing. When loading clay ware it is permissible with all clays except bone china, to place one pot inside another if this is at all possible. Thus small bowls can be placed inside larger ones. However, bear in mind that for a short time during biscuit firing (when the chemically bound water is driven away from the clay), the ware becomes physically weaker than it was in the clay state. You therefore have to be careful not to pack too many pots inside another as the largest pot may give way during the firing. Clay pots can be placed upside down or on their side if this assists tighter packing and there is no increased risk of warping. Lidded pots are normally fired with their lids on to ensure equal shrinkage and subsequent fit and lids may be placed upside down in the biscuit fire if they have high knobs which take up space.

Closed-in shapes such as vases and teapots are comparatively easy to fire because their compact forms have a structural resistance to warping. Cups and bowls are more liable to warp and identical pairs of these are often 'boxed' together, i.e. one on top of the other (rim to rim). In industry, such boxing is, incidentally, often done when the clay ware is put down for final drying – since this helps to avoid warping – and gum arabic solution is used to hold them more firmly. The gum readily burns away during firing.

Large heavy pieces may need shrinkage platforms under them to prevent warping. These are slabs of clay made from the same clay as the pot and which therefore shrink to the same extent. A thin layer of calcined alumina or silica sand between the shelf and the shrinkage platform assists movement during the shrinkage stage.

Finally, the cones should be placed in position and checks made to ensure that they can be seen from the spyhole in the door. With top loaders it is of course necessary to do this when loading the shelves nearest the spyholes as it can not be done when the upper ones are in position.

Loading for Glaze Firing

It is important that glazed pieces do not touch each other during firing as they will stick together. It is therefore necessary to leave a small space between each item. Similarly, items for placing directly onto the kiln shelf must not have any glaze on the underside or they will be firmly stuck in position after firing.

Many pots are placed flat but glaze at the base is avoided by using wax resist during dipping, or is removed by using a damp sponge or a damp piece of felt. With earthenware and other porous wares it is often necessary to glaze the undersides and in this event there are several different kinds of firing support which can be used to keep the ware clear of the kiln shelf. (See photograph on p. 84.) Such supports are inexpensive and it is false economy to repeatedly use the same ones so much that they develop blunt or broken points. A new stilt, for example will hardly leave a blemish on the base of a pot covered with a thin layer of glaze but after several firings may have to be broken away from the pot, leaving unsightly marks which have to be rubbed down.

Pots loaded for biscuit firing

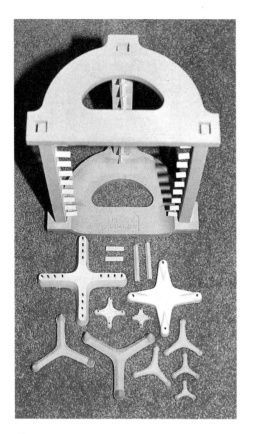

Various ware supports: pin crank, saddle pins and stilts

A further advantage of using stilts or saddles is that they permit some air circulation under the pots. This reduces any temperature variation between the top and bottom of the article and helps to prevent the occurrence of cracking or dunting.

These supports cannot be used for stoneware or porcelain wares however since such wares would tend to squat or deform over them if fired to the normal maturing temperature of these bodies. (In any event, stilts, saddles etc. are not designed for firing above about 1200°C and may themselves deform.) Consequently, it is usual to leave

stoneware and porcelain items unglazed at their base so that they can be set down flat upon the kiln shelf for glaze firings.

You may have noticed three marks on the underside of industrially-made saucers between the rim and the foot ring. These are the three points at which the saucer was supported on special cranks during the glost firing. These cranks, which are very extensively used throughout the industry, are refractory racks into which identical plates or saucers can be very tightly placed. Pin cranks, as they are called, can only be used for glazed ware if the biscuit ware has been fired to a higher temperature than is intended for the glazed ware as otherwise the plates or saucers inside the crank would warp during the glost firing. They can therefore be used to advantage with glazed earthenware, terracotta or bone china wares but not with stoneware or porcelain.

When placing glazed ware into the kiln, hold the pieces firmly; trying to hold the pieces delicately with thumb and finger is much more likely to result in the glaze film becoming damaged unless, of course, the pots are very small. If any glaze is knocked away during handling then apply some more, either touched on with a finger or soft brush, followed by rubbing smooth when dry. It is best to place the props on the shelf before the ware to allow for the space they take up and to ensure correct positioning. With top-loading kilns, be sure the shelf will clear all pots below before lowering it onto the props.

When placing stoneware or porcelain items into the kiln be careful not to place bowls etc. in a position where they closely overhang nearby refractories such as the feet of certain types of kiln prop or cone holders as they may shrink down onto them.

Glost-fired ware load

Some glazes affect others during firing. Glazes containing chromium may cause a pink tinge on nearby tin-glazed wares, or a brown discoloration on zinc ones. Lead glazes placed very close to matt ones may cause some shine. Bright red glazes are especially temperamental and need plenty of space around them. White glazes generally should be kept well away from highly pigmented ones, and so on. With experience you will come to know which glazes need to be kept well away from others for a separate firing.

Don't forget the pyrometric cones and do make sure that when they collapse they will not fall against a pot which has been placed too close to them – a point easy to overlook. Finally, close the door or lid of the kiln and you are ready to begin firing.

Chapter Thirteen
Basic Effects of Heat on Clay, Glazes and Pigments

Clay Bodies

Most terracottas and stoneware clays consist of different clays dug from the ground and which are then blended and purified. Most other clays however are blends of clay with other minerals. A typical white earthenware clay body for example may be made of two or three different ball clays, China clay (kaolin), flint and Cornish stone or feldspar. These are mixed together in liquid form in carefully controlled amounts followed by sieving and magnetting. The purified slip is then pumped to filter presses where surplus water is removed and the filter cakes are then passed to a pugmill which slices and mixes the clay to a very homogeneous, 'plastic' condition. Alternatively, the ingredients in finely powdered form are mixed with water in a batch mixer and then discharged into the pugmill. Either way, the prepared clay from the pugmill is generally referred to as a 'clay body'.

Each of the constituents of prepared pottery clays plays a different role. Ball clays are generally introduced to make the body plastic and to give it good workability. China clays add whiteness to the body and are always appreciably more refractory than ball clays. Flint, as we shall see later, supplies silica and is introduced mainly to develop craze resistance, and feldspar or Cornish stone serves as the flux which melts and holds the other particles together.

When the clay body has been fired it should not be considered as one homogeneous mass however. Reactions in ceramic bodies proceed very slowly and are invariably incomplete so that a state of equilibrium is almost never obtained. The influence of firing time is therefore almost as important as that of temperature. Rapid biscuiting is therefore not recommended since it is seldom cost effective due to greater loss from cracking, distortion, subsequent crazing and bloating problems, and lower fired strength.

Effect of Heat on Clays

Although clay ware should be completely dry before being subjected to a firing process, it is important that the initial firing speed be at a sufficiently slow rate to boil away any traces of pore water without rupturing the ware. Over-quick firing during the first 200°C or so may cause the ware to crack or explode due to steam pressure.

No changes take place in the clay over this initial 'water-smoking' period and up to a temperature around 450°C, but as heating increases progressively higher, fundamental changes occur in the clay substance, in the accessory minerals and in the impurities present as the clay body changes into biscuit.

Around 450°–500°C the 'dehydration' period starts when chemically-bound water begins to dissociate from the clay mineral. By 650°C most of the chemically-bound water has been driven off. Incidentally, the escaping water is quite acidic and can rapidly corrode metal parts of the kiln in contact with it.

Thermal gradients develop in the ware during firing. These are due to the fact that some parts of the ware are nearer to the elements than others and also due to differences in the thickness of the ware. The effect of the kiln shelves also has to be taken into account. The shelf tends to chill the base of a pot standing on it with the result that a temperature gradient from top to bottom of the ware is developed which usually results in the base of such pots being slightly underfired compared with the upper sides. The faster the firing speed the more these thermal gradients become pronounced.

One of the most important phases of biscuit firing, beginning around 450°–500°C, is the burning away of carbonaceous materials present in the clay. Above 600°C, deposits at the surface burn away quite quickly. Less quick is the combustion of organic material below the surface layers, since the air needed for its combustion must penetrate to the interior from the surface and this takes time. Due to this time lag and the presence of thermal gradients in the ware, the burning of organic matter continues through to 900°C and beyond. Indeed, although the bulk is removed by 1000°C much depends upon firing speed and if the all-important range of 600°–1000°C is traversed too quickly, organic matter remaining in the ware may be sealed in by the vitrifying surface layers of the ware. Black coring may then result plus a likelihood of bloating if the subsequent firing is taken to the point where the clay becomes pyroplastic, thereby allowing the pressure generated by gases from the organic matter to create bubbles and bulges in the ware.

Porosity and Shrinkage

The porosity of the ware progressively increases from commencement of firing and reaches a maximum around 800°C. The ware is then as porous as a sponge as it has now lost all its chemically-held water and most of the carbon but no fusion of fluxes has yet occurred. At this stage it is lighter in weight and weaker than when first put into the kiln.

The ware also undergoes slight thermal expansion up to about 600°–850°C (depending on clay type) and then may stabilise a little before sintering and the progressive fusion of fluxes causes firing shrinkage to begin and porosity to decrease. The final fired shrinkage depends, of course, upon body type and firing temperature.

Vitrification

As the ware is taken to higher temperatures – either during high temperature biscuiting or during the glaze firing – the fired porosity of the ware continues to diminish as the ware becomes more dense and shrinks. Fired strength then increases rapidly and would be at a maximum when complete vitrification has been achieved or just a little beyond that point. In practice, full vitrification is almost never achieved; some porosity exists in most well-vitrified bodies although the pore structure may be discontinuous so that the ware becomes impervious to water ingress. Due to the thermal gradients mentioned earlier, pots may have significantly higher porosity in the base than in the side walls, especially with quick firing.

Firing Range

A clay body is correctly fired when it has developed its characteristic strength or degree of vitrification without deforming, and also when it has developed a sufficient coefficient of thermal expansion to enable glazes to be applied and used without crazing. The temperature or, more correctly, the range of temperature at which this stage is reached, varies from one type of body to another and is referred to as the firing range, maturing range, or vitrification point of the clay. Some clay bodies, for example porcelain, will be more or less vitrified when this point has been reached, others such as earthenware and terracotta, will possess an appreciable degree of porosity.

Most craft potters biscuit fire to about 1000°C and this should be considered the minimum. The body is then matured during the glaze firing at a temperature which coincides with the maturing temperature of the clay body in order to prevent crazing of the covering glaze. Industrial potters and hobby ceramicists firing earthenware-type bodies, biscuit fire to the maturing range of the clay and then use a lower temperature glaze firing.

Silica is the most important material in ceramics. Indeed, it is the fundamental element of all clays and glazes. Silica occurs abundantly in igneous rocks and consequently also in feldspar (the decomposition product of igneous rock), in clays, sandstones, flint, and as the mineral quartz. It is present in chemically-combined form as a silicate in clays and most raw materials and also as 'free' silica in the form of sandstone, flint and quartz. Flint and quartz are almost pure silica and are often added in finely ground form to earthenware and porcelain clay bodies to improve craze resistance.

The silica crystals in flint and quartz occur in different forms or modifications and undergo some subtle changes when strongly heated. Some change their form

slightly only to revert to the original form when cooled. Others undergo permanent changes and retain their modified form when cooled. These changes are referred to as silica inversions.

Silica Inversions

The most important crystal modifications of silica are as follows:

alpha quartz $\rightleftharpoons$ beta quartz 573°C

$\downarrow$

alpha cristo- $\rightleftharpoons$ beta cristo- 225°C
balite   balite

Whenever these silica forms change from one to another under the influence of heat, an expansion takes place. Similarly, when free silica is subsequently cooled and beta cristobalite, for example, reverts to alpha cristobalite, a contraction occurs.

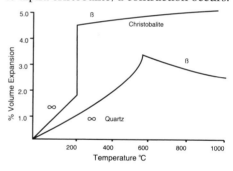

Figure 13.1 Thermal expansion of quartz and cristobalite

When silica is heated it gradually expands until a temperature of 225°C is reached. Here it suddenly expands considerably as the alpha cristobalite content changes to beta cristobalite which has the same chemical composition but larger volume. As heating continues, another sudden expansion occurs at 573°C as alpha quartz changes to beta quartz. However, as heating continues, other forms of silica begin to change into beta cristobalite, this conversion progressing with increasing rapidity as the temperature is raised. If silica is heated above 1200°C for example, a large amount is converted into beta cristobalite. Thus the higher the temperature to which clay body is fired, the more cristobalite is developed within it. This is a very important phenomenon.

As silica is cooled, it gradually contracts until a temperature of 573°C is reached when the beta quartz content reverts to alpha quartz accompanied by a sharp contraction. At 225°C beta cristobalite reverts to alpha cristobalite with an even larger contraction. These expansions and contractions occur every time free silica, or a clay body containing free silica, is heated. They therefore occur during glaze firings as well as biscuit firings.

The formation of an appreciable amount of cristobalite renders pottery clay bodies craze-proof. This is because the beta to alpha cristobalite inversion as the glaze-fired ware is being cooled, suddenly shrinks the biscuit ware causing the glost covering it to be placed in a state of compression. The amount of beta cristobalite produced however depends on the amount of free silica added or present in the body and the maximum temperature to which it is fired. Underfiring is therefore the most common cause of crazing.

Effect of Heat on Glazes

Glazes are suspensions in water of materials which will subsequently melt together when heated to form a glass-like coating. When a glaze is heated, the materials from which it is made begin to combine long before the glaze becomes completely molten. At red heat the glaze particles begin to sinter and as heating continues the glaze gradually softens as the flux content attacks the remaining materials to produce a viscous melt. The process is speeded up by escaping gases from the dissociation of materials and air from between the glaze particles, which produce a stirring action. With continued heating the glaze becomes increasingly more molten and glaze flow develops. Eventually the glaze would become so fluid with further heating that it would run from the ware. The glaze firing range is therefore the range at which a smooth molten glass is developed with sufficient fluidity to allow it to heal small fissures but not so fluid that it will run.

When molten glaze is cooled, it becomes progressively more viscous until, at a temperature of between 800°C and 600°C, depending on the type of glaze, it becomes rigid and ceases to flow. It would not be strictly true to refer to the glaze as now being a solid. Solids have definite melting points: lead, for example, suddenly melts at 327°C. Glazes (and glasses) however do not have a definite melting point but gradually soften over a wide temperature range and they are therefore known as supercooled liquids.

Bubbles and Craters

The gases emanating from the glaze and the body encounter increasing difficulty in escaping as the glaze becomes molten but this then eases as the glaze becomes more fluid. The speed with which these gases bubble through the glaze layer varies with the thickness and fluidity of the glaze layer but when they eventually do reach the surface, they burst and this results in the formation of small craters. The purpose of subsequent heating or 'soaking' of the glaze is to enable it to become just fluid enough to flow and fill in these craters. Soaking, i.e. holding temperature, is useful because it allows bubbling to subside whilst allowing more time for glaze flow to occur and many glaze firing cycles therefore terminate with a 15-30 minute soak period if the low bisque/high glost technique is being followed. Rapid firing and cooling can result in a myriad of gas bubbles being trapped within the glaze or many small pinholes in the glaze surface due to the glaze quickly becoming too viscous to allow the pinholes to flow out.

The Buffer Layer

During firing, the glaze attacks the clay or biscuit surface. This combination of glaze and body at the interface between the two results in a layer known as the buffer layer or reaction layer. A natural consequence of buffer layer formation is the dissolving action of the glaze upon any impurities on the body surface. If the impurity contains a colouring pigment – such as an iron-bearing grog particle – then the action of the glaze produces a larger blotch of colour as the impurity is dissolved into it. The higher the temperature to which the glaze is fired, the stronger the buffer layer formation. This is largely why high temperature glazes are frequently very much more speckled, and also results in crazing of the glaze being much less likely due to the glaze being more effectively 'glued' into position.

Cooling Considerations

Matt glazes, zircon-opacified glazes and various other crystalline glazes are produced by the development of crystals which precipitate from the glaze solution as the glaze cools. The growth of these crystals depends upon several factors but particularly upon the cooling rate. Rapid cooling inhibits crystal development due to the stiffening glaze preventing further growth. As a consequence, matt glazes can fire glossy and zircon-opacified glazes may fire semi-opaque. All crystalline glazes should therefore be slowly cooled from their molten phase so as to allow sufficient time for the required crystallisation to take place.

On the other hand, transparent glazes need rapid cooling for optimum transparency; crystal formation is exactly what is not needed. In practice, however, most glazes have sufficient tolerance, and the cooling rate of most kilns is such that satisfactory results are usually obtained from mixed loads in the same firing. Nevertheless, the rapid cooling rate of very small kilns may demand separating the crystalline glazes and firing these down instead of switching off. Similarly, with large kilns it may be necessary to speed the initial cooling of transparent glazes by taking out the vent or spy plugs for 20 minutes or so and then replacing them.

Below 750°C or so, most glazes are more or less solid and cooling can be as rapid as the ware permits. Limiting factors are the quartz inversion at about 573°C and the cristobalite inversion at 225°C. Because of temperature gradients however, one cannot rely on a temperature reading and it is therefore best to let the kiln cool at an even rate from 650°C down.

The kiln door should be kept closed and no attempt made to force cooling until the ware is below 200°C and preferably much lower still. Bodies with very low free silica do not have the same silica inversion problems and can therefore be cooled down more quickly if necessary.

Effects of Heat on Colouring Pigments

Oxides and Stains

Studio potters make widespread use of various 'oxides' as colouring pigments. These are cheaper than the underglaze colours, glaze stains or body stains preferred by the industrial ceramist. The essential difference between the raw oxides and these prepared stains is that the stains are themselves made from the same oxides mixed with diluents and fluxes and then calcined by firing to high temperature. The calcined colour is then finely ground and thoroughly washed to remove any remaining soluble salts. Underglaze colours produced in this way tend to be very predictable in use and have the advantage that the unfired colour is generally an indication of the fired colour. They also have a significant flux addition which helps to fix the colour firmly onto the biscuit ware (if the colour has been applied to the clay ware or otherwise 'hardened on') and enables the glaze to 'take' more easily. Glaze stains and body stains differ only in that the extra flux is not added but, even so, these are also often used as painting pigments.

The purpose of firing the blends of colorants, diluents and fluxes that make up ceramic stains is to develop a colouring pigment that is more or less inert by removing the gaseous compounds liberated during firing that might otherwise damage the appearance of the ware. Because of this they are not only more predictable in their colour response but there are usually less problems arising in their reaction with any covering glaze.

On the other hand the subtle colour changes that often characterise the use of oxides and carbonates of metals as colouring pigments can add an indefinable character to craft wares. When raw oxides and carbonates are heated, they dissociate in much the same way as do clays and glazes. Manganese oxide and carbonate, for example, release oxygen and carbon dioxide respectively and these gases bubbling through any covering glaze layer often bring traces of manganese with them resulting in an attractive brown dappling in the glaze. A manganese stain would not do this.

Hardening-on

When underglaze colours are applied to clay ware, the subsequent biscuit firing invariably fixes them securely to the ware surface. It is however common industrial practice when underglaze colours are painted onto biscuit ware for a separate hardening-on fire to be carried out at around 750°C. The hardening-on firing serves to fix the colour more firmly to the ware so that there is much less risk of particles of underglaze colour being dislodged during glaze application. It also burns away the media used in colour application and, if the flux content of the colour is compatible, leaves the porosity of the fired, decorated surface similar to that of undecorated areas, enabling a more even application of glaze. Water-based media and gums used in silk screen and pad printing processes generally render hardening-on firings unnecessary however.

Overglaze Colours

In the case of overglaze colours which are applied to fired glazed ware (i.e. 'glost' ware), there are no significant problems arising from firing reactions because they occur on the surface of the glaze. Overglaze colours, often referred to as 'china paints' or 'on-glaze enamels', are similar compositions to underglaze colours except that very low melting point fluxes have to be used. Also, at the lower firing temperature (generally 750°C) of overglaze colours, it is possible to use other colorants which would burn away at higher temperatures. Consequently, the range of fired colour available with overglaze colours is much greater and includes bright reds and oranges from the use of cadmium selenium stains and gold purples which cannot be well-reproduced at high temperatures (although encapsulated cadmium stains are now available to give reasonable reds at stoneware).

In theory, the decoration firing can be very rapid to a temperature which melts the colour onto the glaze and the kiln then cooled. It is, however, important that the medium used in application is well burned away before the colouring pigment melts otherwise the colour can be pinholed and 'frizzled'.

Chapter Fourteen
Craft and Industrial Firing Procedures

When clay ware is fired, the clay body decomposes under the effect of heat and gases are liberated from the dissociation of clay and other minerals and the burning away of volatiles. If this ware is then refired to a temperature lower than that of the biscuit firing, the amount of further decomposition which takes place will be negligible. If, however, the second firing exceeds the temperature of the first, then the clay body will begin to decompose again, creating further generation of gases which, if the ware is glazed, have to escape through the glaze layer.

Earthenware and Porous Bodies

As a result of the above considerations, there is a significant difference in the firing technique used by the craft potter and that generally used by his industrial counterpart when firing earthenware or other porous bodies. Craft potters invariably fire the greenware first in a biscuit firing to a temperature which makes the clay hard yet porous so that a good glaze film is picked up when the ware is dipped into the glaze. This is then glaze fired to a higher temperature than that of the biscuit firing. Industrial potters, on the other hand, fire their greenware to a biscuit temperature which is higher than the subsequent 'glost' firing of the glazed ware.

The advantage of the industrial technique is that the biscuit ware remains relatively inert during the glaze firing and, since there is less disruption of the glaze by bubbles from the substrate, there are generally less defects in the glaze surface. Furthermore, since there is no further shrinkage during the glaze firing, there is little risk of warping. This permits the use of pin cranks to support glazed saucers, plates and dishes of similar shape and diameter to obtain an especially tight packing of these in the kiln. The difference is well-illustrated by considering the way in which say, a thin pencil-like object would be made. The industrial potter would biscuit fire the clay ware to its maturing temperature and during this firing the object would be left lying flat on a batt or other suitable support to prevent distortion. During the glost firing, which would be at a lower temperature, the same object could be supported merely at its two ends with comparatively little risk of distortion. The craft potter producing the same object would find however that it would be likely to distort during the higher temperature glaze firing unless it was supported at other points along its length, which would result in marks being left on the glaze surface. A further advantage of the industrial technique is that if an item is liable to warp it will do

'Silver' S:86 Sculpture kiln with lift-off sections for placing over sculpted item and separate wall-mounted control box containing all electrical controls

so during the higher-temperature biscuit firing and thus will be less loss value than a warped glazed item. For these reasons, the industrial potter therefore biscuit fires earthenware to the maturing range of the clay i.e. 1100°–1160°C, and then uses glazes which require a lower glaze firing around 1060°–1080°C.

Earthenware biscuit fired to its full maturing range, is however, relatively vitreous and is therefore much more difficult to glaze. These problems can be overcome by adding flocculants such as calcium chloride or magnesium sulphate to the glaze (which enable the glaze to adhere to much more vitreous surfaces) but it does demand careful adjustment and/or a particularly efficient dipping technique to prevent glaze runs from developing on the dipped ware. Alternatively, for really vitreous bodies, the industrial potters use spraying techniques to apply the glaze. This, incidentally, is commonly done with bone china (which is almost glass-like after the usual biscuit firing to about 1240°C, cone 7).

The Craft Potter's Approach

The craft potter forgoes the advantages of the industrial technique so that a high porosity can be obtained in the biscuit ware. The craft potter therefore generally biscuit fires clay ware in the range 960°–1060°C (usually 1000°C) at which point most of the volatiles have been burned away but at which little consolidation has taken place. The high porosity then obtained in the biscuit ware enables the glaze to be easily applied by dipping, resulting in a firm but even coat. This ease of glaze application is the principal reason why the low biscuit/high temperature glaze firing technique is adopted.

The glaze used on the low-fired biscuit ware is one which has a firing range which coincides with the firing range of the clay. The glaze firing therefore serves to develop both the body and the glaze at the same time. Thus, for white earthenware, a glaze will be selected which matures in the range 1100°–1160°C, and for stoneware 1200°–1300°C. However, once the temperature of the glost fire exceeds that of the biscuit, extra gases are given off from the body and these have to pass through the glaze layer. These produce extra bubbles in the glaze which burst upon reaching the ware surface, producing pinholes or small craters. In order to allow more time for these bubbles and craters to dissipate, it is desirable to 'soak' the ware i.e. to maintain the final glaze temperature for a short period of time – usually about half an hour – so that the craters in the molten glaze have an opportunity to heal (by glaze flow) before the glaze becomes too viscous as it cools.

It is important to appreciate that, provided you are using compatible glazes and clay bodies, the temperature to which the body is fired controls the degree of craze resistance developed by the ware. Crazing difficulties can sometimes be overcome by firing the glaze a little higher than was done with previous glaze firings and it is often assumed that the increased craze resistance derives from reactions in the glaze due to the extra heat. This is not strictly true; the extra craze resistance is largely due to the increased amount of heat applied to the body via the glaze layer and to better development of the reaction layer between the two.

Once Firing (Raw Glazing)

In addition to the two-fire method (biscuit and glost), ceramic wares can also be

Amaco CP 1024 kiln

fired by a once-firing process. This involves applying glaze to clay ware and then firing this once to a temperature which develops both the body and the glaze at the same time. Once firing is common in the industry (especially for sanitaryware and tiles) but is generally not cost effective for craft ceramic items due to the higher reject rate from glaze blemishes and cracks which more than compensate for any savings made in firing costs. Indeed, most industrial domestic ware remains twice-fired.

Stoneware and Porcelain

The above comments refer to the firing of terracottas, buff, ivory and white earthenware. It is also necessary to fire bone china to its full maturing temperature (1240°C, cone 7) during the biscuit firing as at this temperature the bone china ware deforms so easily that it has to be placed on special setters or buried in calcined alumina. Glazed bone china could not of course be treated in this way and so the high bisque/low glost procedure has to be adopted.

With stoneware and porcelain, the pots would be so vitreous after being fired to full maturing temperature in the biscuit firing that potters invariably would be faced with glaze application problems when using the dipping process. With these wares it is therefore usual to biscuit fire between 950°C and 1000°C (cone 08 to 06) and then to glaze fire in the range 1220°C to 1300°C (cone 6 to 10).

The quality and texture of stoneware and porcelain glazes are, incidentally, often enhanced by the gases which inevitably bubble through from the biscuit ware and also by the reactions which take place between the glaze and the decomposing body. Indeed, much stoneware pottery owes its success and appeal to the glaze effects brought about by a high temperature glost firing.

Chapter Fifteen
Firing the Kiln

It is generally recommended that firings be done at an average rate of between 100° and 140°C per hour. It is true that glost firings – and especially the firing of glost ware decorated with overglaze colours – can be done more quickly than this. Industrial roller hearth furnaces, for example, are used to fire tiles and other wares in less than one hour for the complete firing. There is, however, a great deal of difference between these specially designed fast-fire bodies and glazes using kilns which place heat evenly over the ware surface, and the production situation of the craft potter. With the latter we have pots which are usually not of the same thickness and which generally have not been evenly dried, resulting in the development of various stresses within the structure of the ware. These are added to by stresses arising during firing due to the side of the ware nearest the elements receiving more heat and also to temperature gradients arising between the top and base of a piece due to the effect of the kiln shelf. The faster the kiln is fired, the more pronounced these stresses become and the greater the risk of failure.

It is therefore best to fire at a reasonably steady rate, as above, and only to attempt quicker firings if necessary and in the light of long experience. There is no doubt that wares are most evenly fired when fired slowly. Modern electric kilns are relatively efficient and the saving in cost of an hour or two firing time is marginal when expressed as the extra cost per piece fired – or disappears if there is more faulty ware than before.

The thickness of the pieces is the most critical factor. A suggested schedule of 100° to 140°C would be usual for wares around $\frac{1}{4}$ in. to $\frac{1}{2}$ in. (6 to 13 mm) thick. Thicker wares would demand a slower rate, particularly in the early stages of biscuit firing. It is common practice to select a set firing cycle based upon the experience of the first few firings and then to keep to this for all future firings of similar loads. A typical firing schedule might be: two hours on a low position of the energy regulator with the spyhole and vent plugs out, followed by three hours on a medium position, and then inserting the plugs and switching to high. Skutt recommends leaving the top spyhole open during the entire biscuit firing to ensure good ventilation. Others favour putting in all plugs and closing the vent much earlier. I prefer to close the vent etc. around 550°C when most of the water has been driven away and the kiln is starting to show red.

Schools particularly may have a problem in not having sufficient time to complete a firing. If this is so, the kiln can be set at a low position of the energy regulators overnight so that the kiln will be at a temperature of a few hundred degrees the following morning. The kiln controls can then be reset to finish the firing later that day.

Biscuit Firing

After all the ware has been put into the kiln, the cones set, and the kiln door closed, you are ready to begin firing. The spyholes and vent hole should be left open. If the kiln is being controlled by one or more energy regulators, these should be set at a fairly low setting – normally about 10 to 20 per cent on. If the kiln firing speed is being controlled by a temperature controller, then any energy regulators would normally be switched full on and the controller set to give a firing rate of about 80° to 100°C per hour. This slow firing rate ensures that during the early stages of firing any pore water held inside the clay is allowed to escape unhindered upon conversion to steam.

The temperature in the kiln will now steadily climb and steam (which is generally not seen) will escape from the vent hole. After about two to three hours, the energy regulators can be reset to a medium position (if firing manually), or the temperature controller set to give a firing rate of 100° to 140°C per hour. This setting can be maintained for a further two to four hours.

Towards the end of this period, large volumes of water vapour (from liberation of chemically-held water in the clay) will have escaped from the vent and the kiln may now be showing a dull red inside if the temperature has reached 550°C to 600°C. The vent plug and spyhole plugs can now be inserted and the energy regulators set at 80 to 100 per cent on if manually firing. Otherwise the controller can be left to continue firing at 100° to 140°C per hour. With stoneware clays, it is best to keep to the slower end of this range to help ensure that a maximum amount of carbonaceous material is burned away before shutting off the kiln at about 1000°C. Earthenwares, redwares and porcelains can be fired a little more quickly to the same 1000°C firing temperature, especially if they are thin cast wares.

If the firing speed of the kiln is being controlled manually, checks should be made upon the actual firing speed for, with the regulators turned full on, the kiln will increase its temperature at maximum speed. Some kilns are much more powerful than others and the firing speed may be found to be much too rapid with the energy regulators turned fully on. In that event they should, of course, be set to a lower setting on future firings.

By 800°C the kiln interior will be brightly glowing red. If the kiln is equipped with a temperature indicator this will help to determine the point at which you should start looking into the kiln to check the cones. This would normally be about 20° to 30°C before the first cone is due to collapse. Without a pyrometer you must rely upon glancing into the kiln every 30 minutes or so from bright red heat until the first cone begins to bend. The kiln should be switched off the moment the cone to which the ware is being fired has collapsed.

Ideally, the kiln should be held at the usual biscuit firing temperature of 1000°C for a short soaking period of about 15 to 30 minutes. This helps to even out temperature variances in the kiln and to produce more evenly-fired ware.

If the industrial procedure of high bisque/low glost is being followed then the biscuit firing temperature will be higher: for earthenware normally about 1120° to 1130°C, cone 02 to 01. Again, a soaking period is advisable. With hobby ceramic wares, the biscuit would usually be taken to about cone 04.

With automatic temperature controllers the above firing rates,

Front-loading kiln with elements all round (*Stanton Pottery Supplies*)

finishing temperature and soak period can simply be programmed in. The only manual involvement is inserting the plugs or bungs and checking the cones. Checking the cones is essential since it is these that should determine the end point of a firing. If there is an apparent discrepancy between a cone reading and that of a pyrometer, always be guided by the cone.

Cooling the Kiln

The rate at which kilns cool varies from model to model and also depends upon the temperature, amount of ware and furniture in the kiln. It is best to leave the kiln as it is until the interior has dropped to less than 200°C at which time the door or lid can be 'cracked open' in stages or the vent or spyholes opened. Be wary about having both the vent and the door or spyholes open for this will induce a through draught. Provided the ware is below 200°C this would not normally be a problem with biscuit ware but it is difficult to be sure of the temperature as densely packed areas will be significantly hotter than single pieces with a lot of air around them (e.g. as with a thermocouple probe).

Typical Biscuit Cycle

Energy regulator 10 to 20 per cent on for two hours.
Energy regulator switched to 40 to 60 per cent for three hours.
Vent plug etc. inserted and energy

regulator switched to 80 to 100 per cent setting.

At 1000°C, cone 06, soak for 20 minutes and/or switch off.

Glaze Firing

Each glaze has a maturing temperature to which it should be fired no matter at what temperature the biscuit firing was done. When firing stoneware and porcelain, for example, the glaze firing would normally be done in the range 1240° to 1300°C, cone 7 to 10, the greenware having been biscuit fired around 1000°C.

After packing the kiln as described in Chapter 12, switch the kiln to a low setting to drive away surplus moisture retained by the biscuit ware as a result of glaze application. This may not be necessary if the dipped ware has been thoroughly dried after glazing. The vent and/or spyholes can be left open for the first two hours or so to assist the escape of moisture.

After one to two hours (depending on the thickness and dryness of the ware), switch the kiln to medium or about 50 per cent on the energy regulator or infinite control switch. The vent and spyholes can then be closed and the kiln left on this setting for one hour or so before switching to high. Some ceramicists dispense with the medium position altogether during the glaze firing and switch the kiln to its highest setting at the earliest possible time. This is all right provided that no cracking or dunting of the ware is experienced.

As the kiln temperature approaches the required glaze firing temperature, gas bubbles will still be escaping through the glaze layer and forming craters in the glaze. If the firing has proceeded very rapidly up to this stage, there may not be sufficient time for these craters to heal over before the kiln is switched off and the glaze solidifies. With earthenware it is therefore best to slow down the rate of temperature increase over the last 50° to 100°C or so if the kiln has been fired at a faster rate than about 140°C per hour. With stoneware there is a risk of bloating if the firing speed from 650° to 1000°C exceeds 100°C per hour.

Begin checking the cones about 100°C or so before the finishing temperature and at the glaze firing temperature or appropriate cone, soak the kiln for 15 to 30 minutes and/or switch off. The kiln should then be left to cool until it can be opened and the ware examined. If the glaze surface is pinholed, has an 'eggshell' or 'orange peel' effect, or contains a large number of bubbles, reduce the rate of temperature increase during the later stages of the next firing, or extend the soaking period before switching off.

Cooling

The speed at which kilns cool to unloading temperature after switching off varies widely from one type of kiln to another, but on small- to medium-size kilns is usually similar to the firing time. It is therefore common to leave a kiln tightly closed to cool for about the same length of time as it was fired.

If the kiln takes too long to cool to 750°C, the surface of glossy glazes may become dull and some devitrification may occur. On the other hand, a slow cooling rate is necessary to obtain best results from matt glazes. Consequently, it is occasionally necessary to vary the rate of cooling to suit the type of ware being fired. For glossy glazes, the cooling rate may be speeded by partial or complete removal of the vent plug but this must be replaced before the temperature drops below 800°C to avoid risk of damage to the kiln furniture and the ware load. If such fast cooling is necessary, it usually suffices to remove the vent plug for about 15 minutes and then to replace it. Below 800°C, the kiln should be allowed to cool slowly, especially as the kiln passes the silica inversion temperatures, until the temperature is well below 200°C at which point the door or lid can be 'cracked' open in stages until the ware is cool enough for removal. This involves no more than merely releasing the tight seal around the door at first, followed by slightly opening the door about 20 minutes later. The door must not be flung open whilst the ware is much too hot to handle since ware in the more tightly packed areas may be so hot that it is cracked by the cold air entering.

Significant temperature variations may occur inside a kiln whilst it is cooling and too much reliance should not be placed on the pyrometer reading. Opening up the kiln after a glaze firing to observe the results is one of the thrills of the potters' craft – but it pays to be patient.

I should perhaps conclude this section by stating that it is possible to achieve very satisfactory results in glaze firings merely by switching the energy regulator to a medium or high setting, switching the kiln off when the required temperature has been reached, and opening it up when the kiln has cooled approximately to room temperature. There must be many ceramicists who fire their kilns with complete satisfaction by following this simple and basic procedure. You will however generally be able to obtain even better results if you appreciate what is happening inside the kiln at any particular time and can act as the catalyst in adjusting the firing cycle to make it more appropriate to the requirements of the ware.

Once Firing

With this technique – which is often referred to as 'raw glazing' (although this term more properly refers to a glaze made up of naturally occurring or 'raw' materials rather than synthetic or fritted ones), the clay ware is glazed using a glaze containing an appreciable addition of clay or bentonite (to allow the glaze shrinkage to conform to the pot shrinkage). Since the glaze firing develops both the clay and the glaze at the same time, it is necessary to adopt a firing cycle which combines the slower and careful temperature rise of biscuit firings with the soaking period needed for glost firings. In particular, once-fired products have to be fired very slowly over the 650°–1000°C range when organic materials are being burned away most rapidly. Twice-fired products traverse this range twice at a firing speed of perhaps 100°–140°C per hour. Theoretically, once-fired products should be fired at half this speed over the 650°–1000°C range in order to achieve the same degree of combustion. Some potters hold temperature for an hour or so at around 900°C to facilitate complete burning of the organic matter. Firing should also be slow in the 400°–600°C range when chemically-bound water is being driven away from the clay. If this is done too rapidly, crawling of the covering glaze is likely. Most wares can be once-fired but it is seldom cost effective to do so. This is due to the extra losses which are generally incurred which more than compensate for the savings in having one firing instead of two.

Overglaze Decoration Firing

Generally, the firing of overglaze decorated ware can be done at a faster rate than for other firings. Ideally, the applied decoration should be quite dry

Specially designed for the decoration firing of two sets of sanitary ware, this 27 cubic foot kiln has a 36″ × 36″ × 36″ firing chamber. (*Potclay Kilns Ltd.*)

before firing commences. A firing speed of around 150°C per hour can be aimed at as a reasonable average through the firing, finishing at about 750°C. Faster cycles can be used for simple shapes such as saucers and tiles in cranks but with complex shapes of varying thickness such as some sculptures, a slower cycle might be necessary to avoid the risk of dunting caused by temperature gradients developing in the ware.

Firing should commence with the vent fully open and the energy regulator set at about 20 per cent for the first hour. The energy regulator can then be reset to around 50 per cent and the kiln left at this setting until red heat begins to show in the kiln around 500°–550°C. By then the characteristic odour of burning media should have disappeared. If this is so, the vent plug can be inserted and the energy regulator turned a little higher – perhaps

75 per cent – to take the firing to the required firing temperature (usually 750°C). If the media has not burned away by 550°C, then the vent plug should not be inserted and perhaps the energy regulator should be turned back a little until the smell from the kiln has virtually gone. With an automatic temperature controller, the firing rate can be set at, say 140°C, to the required firing temperature. The vent plug will need to be inserted around 550°C or after the media has burned away.

The required firing temperature varies a little with the type and colour of the overglaze being used. Some colours are best around 780°C, others, particularly some of the reds and oranges, are best around 720°C. An average of 750°C generally works very well and is therefore commonly used. This corresponds to Orton cone 016.

Chapter Sixteen
Special Effects

Reduction

When the atmosphere within a kiln becomes deficient in oxygen, it is referred to as a reduction atmosphere. Under these circumstances, sufficient oxygen cannot be obtained by the materials being fired to enable proper conversions and reactions between them to take place. A consequence is that the constituents of the clays and glazes 'fight' amongst themselves thereby forcing some of them to give up part of the oxygen content they contain. Copper oxide, for example which would normally give a green colour when fired, loses an oxygen atom from the molecule and in that form gives a red, ox-blood colour often known as *sang-de-boeuf*. Similarly, red iron oxide reduces to black iron oxide producing tenmokus and grey-green celadons.

Effects on Elements

There is no doubt that continuous exposure to a reduction atmosphere dramatically lowers the life of Kanthal and all other element wires except silicon carbide. What happens is that the protective alumina coating formed on the elements is progressively removed until the element metal is revealed. Corrosion by the reduction atmosphere then proceeds very rapidly. However, two or three reduction firings are usually necessary before the alumina coating is removed to expose the element metal – and the coating can be restored by carrying out one or two normal firings i.e.

oxidised firings. It is therefore possible to create a reduction atmosphere inside an electric kiln without excessively rapid element failure provided that the protective alumina coating on the elements is not allowed to seriously deteriorate. In practice, this means visually checking the elements after a reduction firing and then carrying out one or two oxidised firings if, as is likely, the elements have lost their characteristic colour. If the reduction atmosphere is of short duration or not very powerful, it may be possible to carry out two or three reduction firings before oxidising ones are necessary.

Even with these precautions however, element life will be lowered compared with that expected from normal oxidised firings but may nonetheless be reasonable. The exact life cannot be determined since it depends upon the degree of reduction, duration time, temperature etc. The characteristic qualities of reduced ceramic wares often enables higher prices to be commanded however and this may compensate for the shorter element life. It has to be said though that if the intention is to regularly produce reduction fired wares, one needs a gas- or oil-fired kiln not an electric one. This applies also to kilns fitted with silicon carbide elements. These are not affected by reduction atmosphere but the high cost of such elements and the voltage regulators etc. needed in conjunction, makes such kilns much more expensive

Crystalline glazed pot by Derek Clarkson

than conventional electric kilns. Similarly, kilns have been made with Kanthal elements inside a muffle tube in order to protect them from a reduction atmosphere, but again the element cost has not proved cost effective.

Formation of Reduction Atmosphere

This can be done by introducing into the kiln sufficient highly-organic materials to burn up most of the oxygen in the kiln atmosphere, leaving little or none for the ware load and creating carbon dioxide and carbon monoxide gas. Charcoal is often used for this and firms such as Amaco and Potclays Ltd, produce optional reduction base units for their top-loading kilns. These consist of a deep, brick base section with one brick which is removable like a sliding drawer. Charcoal is placed in the brick cavity and the brick pushed home. This is repeated at approximately 20-minute intervals. The glaze constituents are in their most reactive state and thus most susceptible to reduction when the glaze is in a molten condition. Sufficient reduction can therefore be obtained by introducing the charcoal as the top temperature is reached, continuing until the kiln is switched off and has cooled to about 800°C.

Moth balls inserted through the spyholes to drop into a suitably positioned container, very efficiently produce a reduction atmosphere but they give off a very toxic gas and also produce a slight glazing effect on brickwork and elements and therefore cannot be recommended. Other methods include a drip feed oil system and, most commonly of all, a gas burner or poker inserted into the kiln with the primary air restricted so that it burns with a yellow flame. Here again, great care is needed to ensure safety and the burner used only above, say 1000°C, when the gas would automatically re-ignite if accidentally turned off and on again. Ideally such burners should nevertheless be fitted with a flame failure control.

Local reduction of the ware can be achieved by adding one to four per cent of very finely ground (300s mesh) silicon carbide to a suitable glaze. One to three per cent of copper oxide or carbonate added to the glaze can then provide a good copper red under normal firing conditions. In practice, it is difficult to achieve the optimum silicon carbide addition to achieve proper reduction and a good glaze surface. Too much silicon carbide can leave the glaze grey and pitted; too little and reduction is not obtained. The optimum amount also varies with the firing cycle.

The use of reduction is usually reserved for stoneware and porcelain wares. At low temperatures, and particularly where low solubility lead glazes are being used, a reduction atmosphere should be avoided for the lead content of the glaze will be reduced, forming a grey discoloration of the glaze. An exception to this is the production of certain lustre glazes by loading the glaze with metallic oxides and then using a reduction atmosphere to form a metallic lustre on the glaze surface.

The characteristic colours produced in glazes by the reduced form of certain materials cannot, incidentally, be obtained by adding these materials already in reduced form to a glaze followed by normal oxidising firing. The oxidised fire readily converts the reduced compounds to their more stable oxidised state.

Crystal Glazes

Most matt glazes and glazes such as the aventurine ones are crystal glazes in the sense that their characteristic effect depends upon the development of tiny (micro) crystals in the glaze. With special glaze design and special firing treatment very large (macro) crystals can be grown in glazes and some of the most beautiful glaze effects are achieved by the careful growth of such crystals.

To achieve these, glazes of very low alumina content are needed to which crystallisers such as zinc, titania, rutile etc. are added together with small quantities of colouring oxides or carbonates. Zinc oxide and silica have a natural tendency to combine in glazes to form the mineral Willemite and most of the crystal patterns on pots are of this mineral. Low alumina glazes produce a very liquid melt and since crystal glazes need to be thickly applied to achieve good crystal growth, much glaze may actually run off the pot during firing. For this reason a biscuit tile or other receptacle is needed beneath each pot and additionally a thick layer of batt wash or other separating agent is needed on the pot base. After firing, the base receptacle is broken away and the pot foot ground to shape.

White-firing bodies – particularly porcelain bodies – are the most suitable for promoting the growth of crystals in a clear matrix and for giving clean, bright colours. The firing schedule for porcelain-based crystal glazes involves firing up to around 900°–950°C at the normal glost firing schedule and then firing quickly up to the glaze firing range (usually 1260°–1280°C) at which point the kiln is shut off. The vent and perhaps also the spyholes are then opened to rapidly lower the temperature to between 1130°–1030°C and the kiln then closed up and held at this temperature. The rapid rise to peak temperature and rapid cooling to less than 1130°C incidentally serves to reduce the amount of glaze running from the ware.

Holding the glaze temperature in the 1130°–1030°C region for a few hours will then allow the growth of crystals from glaze solution. Depending on the glaze, the soak temperature and the results required, the holding period can be anywhere between 30 minutes and six hours or more. The kiln is then shut off and left to cool.

A similar procedure can be used for earthenware crystal glazes. In this case the glaze firing temperatures would usually be in the 1040°–1140°C range and the liquidus point or crystal growth range will usually be in the 960°–820°C range. As with other crystal glazes, the crystals are created from low alumina glazes with crystallisers and colouring pigments as above.

Raku

Raku is a fast-firing process involving the abrupt heating and cooling of bisqued ceramic ware to develop interesting textures and attractive colours. The clay body used has to withstand severe thermal shock and therefore usually contains 30 per cent or so of grog (typically one-third fireclay, one-third ball clay, one-third grog) or is a grogged, low temperature talc body. Biscuit firing at normal firing rate is usually done between 900° and 1040°C dependent upon the body. After glazing, the ware is dried and, using tongs, lifted and placed into a kiln already at a firing temperature around 900°–1100°C. Visual observation of the ware in the kiln reveals when the glaze becomes molten and shiny. The kiln is then opened, the ware gripped and lifted out using tongs and then either air cooled or more commonly buried in sawdust, wrapped in paper etc. to produce a reduction effect on the glaze surface. It's a form of 'instant pottery' that is both fascinating and enjoyable and for this reason it is often the focus social event of many potters' gatherings. Indeed, the Japanese word 'Raku' means 'enjoyment'. The raku process however is also used in a more controlled way to produce unusual finishes on distinctive sculptural or artistic pieces that can command substantial prices.

Small propane-fired kilns are mostly used for raku and these are best. Electric kilns can be used, but ideally the kiln needs to be specially designed for the purpose. The best arrangement is to use a 'top hat' type of kiln where the kiln is supported by a gantry and lowered down over the ware load by a winch. As soon as the glaze has melted, the kiln is winched up to reveal the ware load which then can easily and safely be lifted away and new pots placed into position. Alternative methods include using refractory baffles or strips in front of the elements of front or top loaders to prevent accidental contact of the tongs with the kiln wall or the elements. Naturally, door-operated safety switches are needed or steps must be taken to ensure the kiln is shut off before you reach into it.

Electric kilns tend to be much slower than gas kilns in returning to temperature after the ware has been withdrawn and replaced. This is partly due to the fact that the normal electric kiln has to be switched off when opened whereas a gas-fired raku kiln merely has the burners turned down. The extra temperature change can shorten the life of elements and refractories if severe and the kiln must therefore be closed up again as quickly as possible. Because of the slower response time, electric kilns are not well-suited to multiple raku firings but are fine for the occasional piece.

To minimise heat shock problems the lid or door should be opened only as much as is necessary. Risk of damage can be minimised by loading the ware no closer than 2 or 3 in. (51 to 76 mm) from the wall of the kiln. This will make it easier to grip them with tongs and also give less risk of touching the side of the kiln with molten glaze. Also open and close doors or lids very carefully.

Chapter Seventeen
Some Defects in Fired Ware

Bloating

Rapid firing of stoneware (and occasionally redware or porcelain) between 650°C and 1000°C can leave excess carbonaceous material trapped in the ware. Subsequent firing to the vitrification point of the clay body can then result in the formation of large bubbles or blisters due to the trapped gas expanding the body rather as a child blows bubble gum. Frequently, once-fired ware may bloat but twice-fired ones remain OK due to the longer heat treatment of the latter in the 650°–1000°C range.

Overfiring is also a very common cause of bloating.

Lowering the maximum firing temperature by a cone or so is often an effective remedy whatever the cause.

Bloated ware: section through bloat

Cracks in Biscuit Ware

Cracked biscuit pieces are often best discarded. However, minor cracks on valuable items may be filled with ceramic stopping and the piece then glazed and finished in the usual way. Stopping can be made using a paste of powdered biscuit ware and sodium silicate; or a mixture of powdered biscuit ware, a little glaze, a little glaze binder or gum, and water.

Most biscuit ware cracks originate from cracks or stresses present in the clay ware. Check that drying is not too quick and that large pieces can shrink easily across the surface on which they are placed (a layer of paper or sand often assists). Check that pieces are not physically damaged before they are placed in the kiln. Pieces of varied thickness may warp and crack if not dried carefully. 'S' cracks in the base of pieces are often caused by the outer walls drying first and the base drying afterwards whilst the outer walls are rigid (due to having completed their shrinkage). Consequently the base is then under stress and cracks as it shrinks.

Cutting and fettling tools must be sharp to give smooth cuts on trimmed surfaces although it is often best to finish off with a damp sponge especially if fine cracks develop along the trimmed edges.

Too rapid firing up to 200°C and also 450°–650°C, can cause cracks to form. Very heavy spouts, handles etc., can sometimes crack away if the design is not satisfactory (clay props could be used to prevent such cracking). Similarly, badly supported ware may crack at the point of stress.

Cracks in Glazed Ware: Dunting

Dunts are cracks due to thermal stress or shock which passes right through the article. If the edges of the crack are sharp, it was made during the cooling. If they are rounded or smooth, this indicates the crack occurred during heating. Remedies include slowing the heating or cooling rate, avoiding draughts around the kiln, ensuring that the vent plugs are left in position during cooling, and never force-cooling the kiln. Indeed, with some complex pieces, it may be necessary to slow down the cooling rate by putting the kiln controls onto a low or medium setting and overriding or resetting the temperature controller.

Dunted ware

Especially with complex shapes or with pieces having a large flat base (such as casseroles), it is advisable not to place them flat on the kiln shelf but to use stilts, saddles or other means to lift them slightly clear of the shelf to allow air underneath. This gives a more even firing.

Pinholing in Glazes

Tiny holes or blisters are usually caused by gases given off during the glost firing arising from the biscuit ware, from the glaze itself and from air bubbles trapped in the glaze layer during application. The higher the biscuit firing, the less the amount of gas generated from this source during the glaze firing. The more fluid the glaze when molten or the longer the glaze remains in its fluid molten state, the greater the ability of the glaze to flow to fill in the pinholes in its surface. Raising the firing temperature of an underfired glaze may therefore cure pinholing. 'Soaking' the glaze (i.e. holding glaze firing temperature for $\frac{1}{2}$ hour or so) is a good remedy.

Overfired glaze however can boil and emit bubbles (much as does water when boiling). Too rapid glaze firing may not allow bubbles to clear from the glaze before they become imprisoned as the glaze cools and solidifies (fire slower or 'soak' to cure). Glaze applied much too thinly will result in many tiny pinholes which can be corrected by reglazing and refiring.

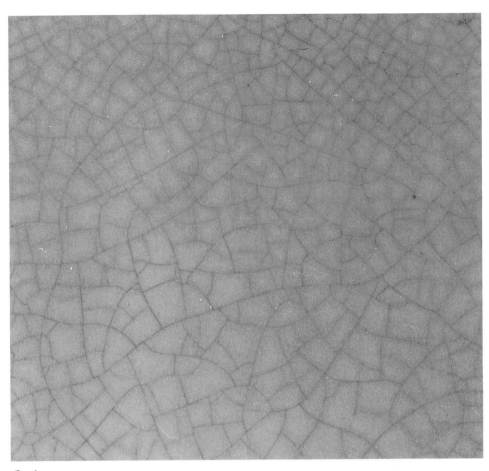

Crazing

Crazing of Glazed Ware

Crazing is caused by a difference in the thermal expansion coefficients of the body and the glaze applied onto it. Matching clay and glaze from the same source of supply is therefore recommended. Fast cooling can promote crazing and ideally the ware should cool slowly in the kiln to room temperature before being removed. Too-thick a glaze also can result in crazing. Crazing can often be corrected by refiring the ware one or two cones hotter than the previous firing and this can be done with ware which crazes some considerable time after being fired.

Generally one should ensure that either during the biscuit or during the glaze firing the ware is fired above the minimum temperature recommended for the clay being used – refer to the manufacturer's specification.

Crawling in Glazes

When a glaze pulls away from the body in firing and forms into balls and drip patterns, the symptom is called crawling, and the remedy is usually a thinner coat of glaze. Too-thick applications of glaze may develop stresses along a curved surface in drying. Cracks may appear in the dried glaze coat, which becomes fissured in firing, and 'crawl' into lumps of glaze, leaving the body bare. Sometimes, a second coat of glaze over the exposed body and refiring may correct the defect. The best corrective measure is a preventative one: namely a thinner glaze application in the first place. Dust or a greasy surface on the biscuit may also cause crawling as can overgrinding of the glaze.

Crawling is very common on once-fired ware and initial heating through to 600°C must be very slow to avoid this, the glaze tending to crawl due to over-fast release of steam from the clay body.

Glaze Craters

Craters are often due to underfired glaze and can be remedied by dabbing glaze into the craters and refiring to a hotter temperature. If, however, due to overfired glaze the craters need grinding level, paint over them with glaze and refire to the correct temperature.

Other Glaze Surface Problems

A shiny glaze which fires dull is probably underfired.

Matt glazes which fire shiny have probably been overfired or in some cases, cooled too quickly over the first 200°C or so after the kiln is switched off (the remedy is then to 'fire-down').

Matt glazes too thinly applied may also fire shiny. This application may result in opaque glazes becoming semi-opaque (also with too quick cooling over the first 200°C).

Spit Out

Spit out occasionally occurs when overglaze colours are fired onto glost earthenware. Moisture trapped inside the ware is forced out causing a mass of minute blisters in the glaze and giving a glasspaper-like feel to the glaze surface.

There is little that can be done during the firing process to avoid this. Affected pieces may sometimes be reclaimed by refiring the piece to glaze firing temperature and then redecorating. Sometimes grinding away of the glaze from a small area on the back of the piece will allow trapped steam to escape there instead of bursting through the glaze. The ground area can then be painted with a clear enamel flux to seal it when fired. Slow, low temperature firings may be successful in driving away the trapped moisture prior to decoration. The only real remedy though is one of prevention by seeing that only new ware is decorated, or decoration is confined to vitrified wares such as bone china and porcelain.

Faded Transfer Decals

Check the transfer manufacturer's recommendation. Fading is generally due to overfiring but occasionally also to underfiring. Little can be done to save an overfired transfer.

Further Information

Ceramic Faults and their Remedies, by H. Fraser published by A & C Black.

Chapter Eighteen
Maintenance and Repair

General

The greatest contribution to the satisfactory performance and life of a kiln undoubtedly is reasonable care and attention during use, particularly in relation to elements and brickwork. Ideally, the kiln interior – and especially the element grooves – should be cleaned after firing or at least at frequent intervals. A vacuum cleaner is the safest and most efficient way of doing this and, with care, all dust or debris accumulated during firing can be removed without contacting the element spirals or causing abrasion to brickwork. Obviously, the kiln should be switched off and isolated before carrying out this work. At the same time, any glaze spots on the kiln shelves, props, side walls or kiln base should be removed also as it will remelt and spread on the next firing. A sorting tool or small cold chisel is useful for this. Check the shelves for cracks and touch in or recoat with batt wash if necessary.

It is recommended that kilns be serviced at regular intervals. Some suppliers suggest a preventive maintenance check after six months use and a full service after one year but kilns in heavy use may need more frequent checks than this. With some suppliers the warranty is voided if the recommended service intervals are not followed.

Brickwork

Some surface cracking on hot-face brickwork may arise during use. Such cracking is quite common, especially when kilns are rapidly fired but this is not detrimental to kiln performance and can generally be ignored. If deep, wide cracks develop these can be filled with refractory cement using a small pointed trowel. Similarly, small holes may be filled with cement. Larger holes should be squared out, vacuumed and filled with hot-face brick shaped to the size of the hole and cemented. Refractory, hot-face bricks are easily cut with a coarse wood saw or hacksaw blade, or similar tool.

It is essential that refractory bricks are a tight fit with thin joints. The applied cement mortar should not be thicker than $\frac{1}{16}$ in. (1.55 mm) and all excess cement must be removed, especially where it may come into contact with elements. To obtain the tightest fit it is generally best to cut a replacement section about $\frac{1}{16}$ in. oversize and then to rub down to a precise fit with a coarse carborundum stone. It is often preferable to 'dovetail' replacement brick sections which involve element channels so that they will securely hold with perhaps just a minimum of cement mortar at the lower surface away from the element contact face.

When the cement is dry the kiln can be fired in the normal way.

Elements

Damage Due to Element Failure

On occasions following the failure of a heating element, arcing may occur between the separated ends of the element resulting in a deposit of slag in the refractory brickwork. This slag must be removed or early failure of the new element is likely. Small deposits of slag can be picked up or gouged out using a knife or screwdriver, and the cavity filled with brick dust or a mixture of dust with a little refractory cement. Alternatively, zircon and China clay mixtures can be used but not fireclay, ball clay or other materials containing iron as they will attack the elements at high temperature.

If the element groove is broken or burned, the damaged portion of brickwork will require replacement.

Element Life

To obtain the best life from elements, they should receive two 'clean air' firings (test or bisque firings) to build up a reasonable protective coating before being submitted to glaze firings. Generally they should be kept as free from harmful fumes as possible and proper venting of the kiln is therefore important. Element life is also assisted by use of a soft brush or vacuum cleaner (as previously mentioned) to keep the element grooves as clean as possible, taking care not to disturb the elements which will likely be in a brittle state.

Suspected Faulty Elements

Visual inspection will probably identify an element which has failed. Look for burn marks or slag on the brickwork where arcing may have occurred at the break point. With top loaders it is often difficult to inspect the elements low down in the kiln but use of a hand mirror held at a suitable angle close to the element groove enables the image to be inspected and one to see right into the groove.

If a break cannot be seen, the faulty element can be located by switching on the kiln for a few minutes, then switching off and feeling the warmth (or lack of it) by touching each element. If the faulty element appears to be intact on closer inspection, it is likely that there is a defective connection at the element tail. In this event, the mains supply to the kiln must be disconnected *and the fuse removed*. The rear connection cover or switchbox on the kiln can then be removed to provide access to the element connections. Inspection, or a gentle pull on the connector attached to the failed element, will usually reveal the problem. However, since the failed element will likely be one of several wired in a series, it will be necessary to check each member to determine the faulty one.

Sometimes slow firing is due to the general ageing of the elements. Progressive deterioration and corrosion of the elements causes increased electrical resistance resulting in less current drawn and a gradual reduction in firing speed. Low voltage also will cause slower firing so it is necesseary to check the voltage of the supply with the kiln full on to see if the problem is a voltage one. If the supply voltage is correct and the elements are intact but old, it is likely that slow firing can only be corrected by replacing the elements.

Tightness of Screw Connections

Electricity loosens screws. Whenever a connection panel or switchbox is removed to check or replace elements, it is advisable to check the tightness of all element connections and any other mains power connections such as those on the contactor(s).

Replacing Faulty Elements

a) *Front-loading kilns*
   Determine which element has failed
   (see above) then:

1. Switch off the mains and remove main
   fuse or plug.
2. Remove the connecting box cover or
   switchbox cover to the elements.
3. Disconnect the faulty element and
   withdraw it from inside the kiln.
4. Check the element support groove in
   the kiln. It must be complete and
   unbroken. Every piece of burnt brick,
   slag etc. must be completely removed
   and the groove made good followed by
   vacuum cleaning or brushing out.
5. Ensure that the replacement element
   will lie flat in its grooves when the
   element tails are inserted through the
   lead-in holes at the rear of the kiln.
   Adjust if necessary but avoid
   stretching the element. If possible,
   avoid the use of pliers since the surface
   of the wire can be damaged which will
   result in premature breakdown.
6. At the connection chamber or
   switchbox, pull the element tails
   through the back of the kiln until the
   coil butts up to the back wall and
   carefully bend each tail through 90° so
   that when the connector is fitted into
   the tail, it does not lie in the path of
   any hot gases which may pass
   through the lead-in holes. Trim the tail
   to the correct length and secure the
   connector firmly onto the element tail.
7. Gently stretch the 'hairpin' element
   over the grooved kiln bricks to locate it
   into position. Do not stretch the
   element before fitting as over-
   stretching will cause the element to be
   slack in the grooves and it is important
   that it should be in tension.

8. Make sure that all electrical
   connections are properly completed
   and with the electricity supply still
   switched off, check that there is an
   adequate earth wire connection to the
   kiln case and that this provides good
   earth continuity. Check that the fuses
   are of the correct rating.
9. Replace connection chamber or
   switchbox cover and fuses. Switch the
   kiln on and check correct functioning.

Top-loading kilns
Proceed as for front-loading kilns for steps
1, 2, 3 and 4 and then:

5. Bend the element tail to the correct
   angle enabling it to be inserted
   through the brickwork lead-in hole
   whilst allowing the element to lie
   correctly in the element groove.
   Working around the element groove,
   place or feed the element into
   position ensuring that it is pushed
   right to the back of its groove.

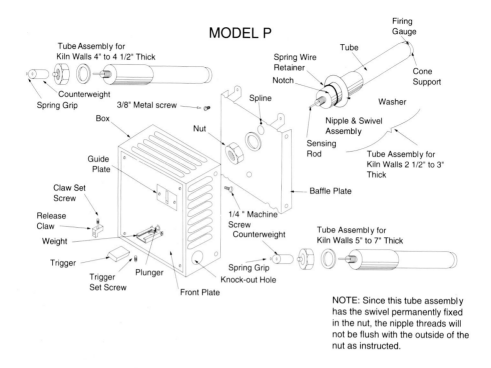

MODEL P

Tube Assembly for Kiln Walls 4" to 4 1/2" Thick

Firing Gauge

Tube

Spring Wire Retainer

Notch

Cone Support

Counterweight

Spring Grip

3/8" Metal screw

Spline

Washer

Box

Nut

Nipple & Swivel Assembly

Guide Plate

Sensing Rod

Tube Assembly for Kiln Walls 2 1/2" to 3" Thick

Claw Set Screw

Release Claw

Baffle Plate

Weight

1/4 " Machine Screw

Trigger

Counterweight

Tube Assembly for Kiln Walls 5" to 7" Thick

Trigger Set Screw

Plunger

Spring Grip

Front Plate

Knock-out Hole

NOTE: Since this tube assembly has the swivel permanently fixed in the nut, the nipple threads will not be flush with the outside of the nut as instructed.

MODEL K

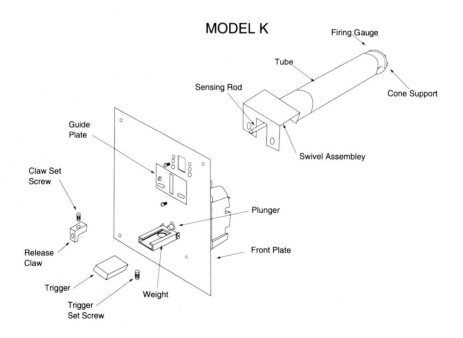

Firing Gauge

Tube

Sensing Rod

Cone Support

Guide Plate

Swivel Assembley

Claw Set Screw

Plunger

Release Claw

Front Plate

Trigger

Weight

Trigger Set Screw

Figure 18.1 Kiln Sitter: exploded view

6. The element will generally be found to be a little longer than its groove so that when the remaining element tail is bent and inserted into its lead-in hole, a 'loop' forms.

7. Push the loop into position thus causing the element to bulge out of its groove a little further along. If this is then pushed home and one works along the element in this way, it should be found that the bulge becomes progressively smaller until eventually the element lies fully positioned at the back of its groove.

   Sometimes an element may be found to be a little short or too long. If short, gently stretch it but not all from one area; if too long slightly compress it by hand but again not all in one area.

8. At the switchbox, carefully bend the element tails away from the lead-in tubes, snip off excess tail and fasten securely into the element connectors.

9. With the electrical supply still switched off, check that all electrical connections have been properly made; that there is an adequate earth with good continuity, and that the fuses are correctly rated.

10. Replace the switchbox cover and mains fuses. Switch the kiln on and check for correct working.

Kiln Sitter Maintenance

Due to heat, corrosion or mechanical wear, a Kiln Sitter may get out of adjustment over the course of several firings. Also, the repeated fall of the weight could cause the trigger to creep so that a correctly bent cone is not obtained. To ensure consistent firing, it is recommended that the various adjustments and checks detailed in the Dawson Manual are carefully repeated every 20 firings or so.

Sluggish movement of the sensing rod may eventually occur due to accumulation of residue or corrosion of the swivel. If this happens, remove the claw from the sensing rod, slacken the swivel nipple (if fitted) and push the sensing rod in and out of the swivel assembly for a few centimetres whilst rotating the sensing rod between the fingers. If this does not eliminate the problem, the nipple and swivel assembly must be replaced. Free and easy movement of the sensing rod should be checked before each firing.

Incidentally, Dawson recommend that the top side spyhole be left open during firings. This is because if the kiln is not properly vented, gases may be forced out through the Kiln Sitter tube. This may lead to the pivot point corroding and eventually cause the sensing rod to stick in position during firing, causing an overfire. With the top spyhole open, outside air goes through the Sitter and out the spyhole, thus minimising corrosion problems at the pivot point.

Eventually the sensing rod wears thinner at the working end. It can then be reversed but it is better to replace it. It is best also to replace the cone supports if any molten or non-removable material is stuck to them (although sometimes this can be softened with a blow torch and flicked away).

Pyrometer Maintenance

Apart from checking that the instrument correctly reads room temperature (and not zero) when the kiln is at room temperature and that the instrument gives a consistent approximation to cone readings during firings, there is little that can be done in the way of maintenance.

Any marked change in performance should be discussed with the supplier and the instrument returned for servicing if necessary. Manufacturers recommend they should be periodically service checked and recalibrated.

Trouble-Shooting

Warning *If maintenance is necessary, always ensure that mains electricity has been completely isolated before removing any connection chamber or switchbox cover.*

1. Kiln Will Not Operate

A. If red power-on light does not come on this could signify:
   a. Blown fuse in isolating switchbox.
   b. Defective connection or fault in power supply to the kiln.
   c. Faulty bulb or neon in power-on light (but this in itself would not prevent the kiln from operating).

B. If red power light is on:
   a. Check that door or lid is closed and any safety switch is correctly set.
   b. Check that energy regulators are switched on.
   c. Check that timer on Limit Timer is set.
   d. Check temperature controller not set or faulty.
   e. Possible blown fuse (normally 3 amp) on secondary circuit.
   f. Poor fuse or fuseholder connection.
   g. Faulty safety switch to door or lid.
   h. Faulty contactor or wire connection.
   i. Failure of one or more elements or connections in each element circuit.
   j. Defective neutral connection at the kiln. (This often causes the power-on light to be dimmer or to flicker.)

2. Kiln Fires Too Slowly

   a. Failure of one or more elements.
   b. Faulty energy regulator.
   c. Low voltage.
   d. Aged elements.
   e. Failure of one phase in multiphase supply situation. Check supply fuses.

3. Kiln Fires Unevenly

   a. Failure of element(s).
   b. Kiln loaded very unevenly.
   c. If base is too hot, lift bottom kiln batt higher from base elements.
   d. Overlarge kiln batts. There should be good clearance all round between shelf and kiln walls.
   e. Worn vent plug or door/lid seal allowing cold air to enter.
   f. Uneven aged elements, especially some new with some old elements.
   g. One energy regulator faulty (where several fitted to kiln).

Note that with kilns fitted with several energy regulators, the energy regulator controlling the hottest zone can be switched to a lower setting than the others in order to pass less energy into the hot zone and thus compensate for temperature variance.

4. Kiln Shuts Off Prematurely

   a. Controller incorrectly set or faulty.
   b. Poor connections in thermocouple circuit or faulty thermocouple.
   c. Incompatible instrument and thermocouple e.g. type K thermocouple with type R calibrated instrument.
   d. Sitter Timer set to short time (in this event the Sitter weight will not have fallen and the Sitter cone will still be in position).

Overfired kiln. The kiln furniture has distorted and collapsed causing some damage to the side walls and the base elements to overheat and fail

e. Wrong cone selected for Sitter.

f. Electrical noise or spiking affecting power supply to controller. Ensure capacitor fitted to contactor holding coil.

5. Kiln Overfires

a. Thermocouple head or cold junction overheated.

b. Thermocouple wires crossed or insufficient immersion into kiln.

c. Incompatible instrument and thermocouple type, e.g. type S thermocouple with instrument calibrated for type R.

d. Faulty pyrometer.

e. Wrong cone in Sitter.

f. Badly adjusted Kiln Sitter.

g. Sitter sensing rod or counterweight prevented from falling.

h. Contactor seized.

6. Kiln Does Not Shut Off

a. Contactor seized.

b. Faulty temperature controller.

c. Short-circuited compensating cable or thermocouple.

Chapter Nineteen
Safety Considerations

There are three main areas of concern when reviewing the safety of electric kilns. Obviously, the major one is that of electrical safety but we also need to be aware of fume problems and also, heat problems from risk of burning by contact with hot exterior surfaces.

Electrical Safety

In the UK it is a mandatory requirement that power to electrical elements is isolated whenever a lid or door is opened. The means by which this is done has to be 'fail-safe' which rules out the use of microswitches to cut off power to the holding coil of the contactor. This is because contactors can seize-on so that power to the kiln is continued even though the holding coil is not energised. Also, holding coils are released by the action of springs which can fail. Wherever springs are used in safety switches, the latter must be wired so that if a spring fails, the power to the elements is off not on i.e. they are wired fail-safe. Usually a trapped key system is used, utilising a switch which directly carries the full current of the kiln and which is mechanically activated.

If the elements are not exposed (i.e. muffle construction) then such safety switches are not necessary. Similarly, if elements are held in special element channel holders – where access to the elements is via a narrow slot, too narrow for a finger to pass through, then safety

switch isolation of the elements is usually not needed. Indeed, there is a 'finger test' that is sometimes used to determine whether elements or live contacts are sufficiently inaccessible.

Power cables should not be allowed to lie against the kiln or to come into contact anywhere with the sides and top. It is best to run them inside a flexible conduit which permits the kiln to be moved forwards for servicing needs etc.

An extension cable should never be used to bring power to the kiln. It is better to relocate the kiln or the electrical outlet. Improperly sized extension cables can overheat and be a fire hazard. Keep power cables away from the hot surface of the kiln.

Safety switch. When rotated through 90° to switch on, the spindle (attached to door bracket) cannot be withdrawn through the rectangular slotted plate attached to the kiln fascia or switchbox

It is important that covers to electrical switchboxes to kept properly secured. This may appear to be stating the obvious but the writer has on more than one occasion attended kilns which have all electrical safety devices on the front, but the rear connection chamber panel not secured to the kiln.

Whenever kilns are installed, it is necessary to ensure that there is good earth continuity and this should be routinely checked as part of the routine maintenance and service procedure. The security of incoming mains live and neutral connections at the kiln should also be checked at the same time.

Fuses are important and must be of the correct rating if they are to do the job they are designed to do.

Fume Problems and Ventilation

When ceramic products are fired, various gases are given off. In the case of biscuit firings these consist of water vapour arising from the dissociation of clays and other minerals mixed with traces of a variety of noxious materials such as sulphur dioxide and fluorine. There may also be some smoke arising from the burning away of carbonaceous materials. A similar situation arises with glaze firings except that there is a lower volume of gases but they are of greater variety and toxicity. Some of these are quite hazardous and a few – such as lead fume from fritted lead glazes – especially so. However the hazard is lowered on account of the air dilution factor of that fraction which escapes from the kiln and it is probably that the concentration of noxious gases in an unventilated room will be of similar hazard to that encountered from traffic fumes when walking down a very busy high street.

Evidence of fume discharge from kilns incidentally is often revealed by adjacent glass windows gradually becoming opaque. This is due to fluorine from clays and glazes combining with water vapour in the room to form hydrofluoric acid. This attacks the silica in window glass and the glass progressively becomes etched.

Because of the fume hazard it is best for the kiln to be positioned in a well-ventilated, separate room. Ventilation can be by windows which open on two sides to give cross ventilation or by a small powered fan fitted into a wall or window of the kiln room and exhausting to outside atmosphere. If a fan is used, it is important to realise that an equivalent amount of air must be allowed to enter the room to replace that which is removed, otherwise the action of the fan will be ineffective. Consideration should also be given to the exact position of the fan: it obviously should not be mounted where it causes air from around the kiln to cross the location of people in the room on its way to the fan.

If good room ventilation is not available, the kiln should have an extraction system fitted to the kiln. This can be a canopy which completely envelops the top of the kiln and projects forward above the door to catch gases leaking upwards from the door area, the canopy being fitted with an exhaust flue or motorised fan exhausting to outside atmosphere.

The Orton Vent and Skutt Environment systems are good also. With these, small holes drilled through the lid or roof of the kiln admit clean air to replace the noxious gases which are drawn out of the firing chamber via small holes in the base of the action of a motorised fan. These gases are then taken to outside atmosphere via a flue pipe. Versions are available for both front and top loaders.

Heat Problems

The exterior surface of kilns can become very hot. In the case of top-loading kilns the temperature can exceed 200°C which is twice as hot as boiling water. Generally, you will notice the heat and back off but discomfort levels and pain thresholds can vary. Particular consideration must be given to handicapped people whose awareness levels, and general mobility, may result in burns and damage, and also to inquisitive children. Such people must be prevented from contacting hot kilns and provision of a kiln cage or ideally, siting the kiln in a separate room must be considered and indeed is essential if such persons might contact the kiln. Front-loading kilns – especially those with thick insulation and double skin panels – are preferable to top loaders if external temperature is an important consideration.

Be careful when handling spyhole plugs. Use a glove or mitt. When viewing cones, protective eye wear or use of a cone viewer is recommended. Also be very wary of the lid handles of top loaders which can become extremely hot when the lid is cracked open and heat strikes them.

Ceramic Fibre

Refractory Ceramic Fibre (RCF) is a man-made vitreous (silicate) fibre (MMVF) and consists of alumino silicate fibres, many being fine enough to be inhaled and deposited in the lungs. European legislation (CHIP 98) has classified all such fibres (and including mineral wools) as 'Irritant' but most RCF fibres are also classified as carcinogenic, category 2.

The new regulations are not a ban on use – and RCF should not be compared with asbestos – but result in more stringent control measures applying to avoid inhalation of ceramic fibres. Such control measures include damping with water and generally preventing fibre liberation into workrooms during handling.

Alternative materials include brick and RCF made with coarser fibres, or alumina fibre, but these fibres respectively have a lower service temperature or much higher cost.

Location

Kilns ideally should be in a separate room and sited on a level surface that will not be damaged by heat. A masonry or concrete floor is recommended.

Kilns should be positioned so that there is free air movement all round the kiln and the kiln should be at least 6 in. (15 cm) from any wall. The ceiling or roof should be at least 30 in. (76 cm) above the kiln but these dimensions would need to be increased if either the walls or ceiling are of combustible materials. With combustible ceilings, these can be protected by a heat-resistant board fixed with a 2 in. (5 cm) air gap between the board and the ceiling in the area immediately above the kiln.

Kilns should be sited so as to permit access for servicing or to enable them to be moved to permit such servicing.

Other Precautions

An emergency shut-off procedure notice should be prominently positioned in the kiln room and clearly indicate the location of the kiln isolator.

Ensure that kilns are checked at the appropriate time to see that they have correctly shut-off and afterwards manually turn all switches to off.

Do not use a kiln for other than its intended purpose. Unless specifically designed for it, do not use it for raku or salt firings.

Have the kiln regularly serviced.

Thermocouple Reference table

Absolute thermocouple e.m.f. in microvolts.   Reference junction at 0°C

K = Chromel/Alumel   R = Platinum $-$ 13% Rhodium/Platinum   S = Platinum $-$ 10% Rhodium/Platinum

°C	K	R	S	°C	K	R	S	°C	K	R	S
0	0	0	0	550	22772	5021	4732	1100	45108	11846	10754
10	397	54	55	560	23198	5132	4832	1110	45486	11983	10872
20	793	111	113	570	23624	5244	4933	1120	45863	12119	10991
30	1203	171	173	580	24050	5356	5034	1130	46238	12257	11110
40	1611	232	235	590	24476	5469	5136	1140	46612	12394	11229
50	2022	296	299	600	24902	5582	5237	1150	46985	12532	11348
60	2436	363	365	610	25327	5696	5339	1160	47356	12669	11467
70	2850	431	432	620	25751	5810	5442	1170	47726	12808	11587
80	3266	501	502	630	26176	5925	5544	1180	48095	12946	11707
90	3681	573	573	640	26599	6040	5648	1190	48462	13085	11827
100	4095	647	645	650	27022	6155	5751	1200	48828	13224	11947
110	4508	723	719	660	27445	6272	5855	1210	49192	13363	12067
120	4919	800	795	670	27867	6388	5960	1220	49555	13502	12188
130	5327	879	872	680	28288	6505	6044	1230	49916	13642	12308
140	5733	959	950	690	28709	6623	6169	1240	50276	13782	12429
150	6137	1041	1029	700	29128	6741	6274	1250	50633	13922	12550
160	6539	1124	1109	710	29547	6860	6380	1260	50990	14062	12671
170	6939	1208	1190	720	29965	6979	6486	1270	51344	14202	12792
180	7338	1294	1273	730	30383	7098	6592	1280	51697	14343	12913
190	7737	1380	1356	740	30799	7218	6699	1290	52049	14483	13034
200	8137	1468	1440	750	31214	7339	6805	1300	52398	14624	13155
210	8537	1557	1525	760	31629	7460	6913	1310	52747	14765	13276
220	8937	1647	1611	770	32042	7582	7020	1320	53093	14906	13397
230	9341	1738	1698	780	32455	7703	7128	1330	53439	15047	13519
240	9745	1830	1785	790	32866	7826	7236	1340	53782	15188	13640
250	10151	1923	1873	800	33277	7949	7345	1350	54125	15329	13761
260	10560	2017	1962	810	33686	8072	7454	1360		15470	13883
270	10969	2111	2051	820	34095	8196	7563	1370		15611	14004
280	11381	2207	2141	830	34502	8320	7672	1380		15752	14125
290	11793	2303	2232	840	34909	8445	7782	1390		15893	14247
300	12207	2400	2323	850	35314	8570	7892	1400		16035	14368
310	12623	2498	2414	860	35718	8696	8003	1410		16176	14489
320	13039	2596	2506	870	36121	8822	8114	1420		16317	14610
330	13456	2695	2599	880	36524	8949	8225	1430		16458	14731
340	13874	2795	2692	890	36925	9076	8336	1440		16599	14852
350	14292	2896	2786	900	37325	9203	8448	1450		16741	14973
360	14712	2997	2880	910	37724	9331	8560	1460		16882	15094
370	15132	3099	2974	920	38122	9560	8673	1470		17022	15215
380	15552	3201	3069	930	38519	9589	8786	1480		17163	15336
390	15974	3304	3164	940	38915	9718	8899	1490		17304	15456
400	16395	3407	3260	950	39310	9848	9012	1500		17445	15576
410	16818	3511	3356	960	39703	9978	9126	1510		17585	15697
420	17241	3616	3452	970	40096	10109	9240	1520		17726	15187
430	17664	3721	3549	980	40488	10240	9355	1530		17866	15937
440	18088	3826	3645	990	40879	10371	9470	1540		18006	16057
450	18513	3933	3743	1000	41269	10503	9585	1550		18146	16176
460	18938	4039	3840	1010	41657	10636	9700	1560		18286	16296
470	19363	4146	3938	1020	42045	10768	9816	1570		18425	16415
480	19788	4254	4036	1030	42432	10902	9932	1580		18564	16534
490	20214	4362	4135	1040	42817	11035	10048	1590		18703	16653
500	20640	4471	4234	1050	43202	11710	10165	1600		18842	16771
510	21066	4580	4333	1060	43585	11304	10282				
520	21493	4689	4432	1070	43968	11439	10400				
530	21919	4799	4532	1080	44349	11574	10517				
540	22346	4910	4632	1090	44729	11710	10635				

Wire Gauges

Standard Wire Gauge (British)		Gauge No.	Brown & Sharpe Gauge (AWG or B & S)	
dia. inch	dia. mm		dia. Inch	dia. mm
0.4000	10.160	4–0	4.600	11.684
0.3720	9.449	3–0	0.4096	10.404
0.3480	8.839	2–0	0.3648	9.266
0.3240	8.230	0	0.3249	8.252
0.3000	7.620	1	0.2893	7.348
0.2760	7.010	2	0.2576	6.543
0.2520	6.401	3	0.2294	5.827
0.2320	5.893	4	0.2043	5.189
0.2120	5.385	5	0.1819	4.620
0.1920	4.877	6	0.1620	4.115
0.1760	4.470	7	0.1443	3.665
0.1600	4.064	8	0.1285	3.264
0.1440	3.658	9	0.1144	2.906
0.1280	3.251	10	0.1019	2.588
0.1160	2.946	11	0.09074	2.305
0.1040	2.642	12	0.08081	2.053
0.0920	2.337	13	0.07196	1.828
0.0800	2.032	14	0.06408	1.628
0.0720	1.829	15	0.05707	1.450
0.0640	1.626	16	0.05082	1.291
0.0560	1.422	17	0.04526	1.150
0.0480	1.219	18	0.04030	1.024
0.0400	1.016	19	0.03589	0.912
0.0360	0.914	20	0.03196	0.812
0.0320	0.813	21	0.02846	0.723
0.0280	0.711	22	0.02535	0.644
0.0240	0.610	23	0.02257	0.573
0.0220	0.559	24	0.02010	0.511
0.0220	0.508	25	0.01790	0.455
0.0180	0.457	26	0.01594	0.405
0.0164	0.417	27	0.01420	0.360
0.0148	0.376	28	0.01264	0.321
0.0136	0.345	29	0.01126	0.286
0.0124	0.315	30	0.01003	0.255
0.0116	0.295	31	0.008928	0.227
0.0108	0.274	32	0.007950	0.202
0.0100	0.254	33	0.007080	0.180
0.0092	0.234	34	0.006305	0.160
0.0084	0.213	35	0.005615	0.143
0.0076	0.193	36	0.005000	0.127
0.0068	0.173	37	0.004453	0.113
0.0060	0.152	38	0.003965	0.101
0.0052	0.132	39	0.003531	0.090
0.0048	0.122	40	0.003145	0.080
0.0044	0.112	41		
0.0040	0.102	42		
0.0036	0.091	43		
0.0032	0.081	44		
0.0028	0.071	45		
0.0024	0.061	46		
0.0020	0.0508	47		
0.0016	0.0406	48		
0.0012	0.0305	49		
0.0010	0.0254	50		

Kanthal AF Wire

To obtain resistivity at working temperature multiply by the factor C_t in the following table:

°C	20	100	200	300	400	500	600	700	800	900	1000	1100	1200	1300	1400
C_t	1.00	1.00	1.01	1.01	1.02	1.03	1.04	1.04	1.05	1.05	1.06	1.06	1.06	1.06	1.07

Diameter mm	Resistance Ω/m 20°C	cm²/Ω 20°C	Weight g/m	Surface area cm²/m	Cross sectional area mm²	Diameter mm
12.0	0.0123	30700	809	377	113	12.0
10.0	0.0177	17800	562	314	78.5	10.0
9.5	0.0196	15200	507	298	70.9	9.5
8.0	0.0277	9090	359	251	50.3	8.0
7.5	0.0315	7490	316	236	44.2	7.5
7.0	0.0361	6090	275	220	38.5	7.0
6.5	0.0419	4870	237	204	33.2	6.5
6.0	0.0492	3830	202	188	28.3	6.0
5.5	0.0585	2950	170	173	23.8	5.5
5.0	0.0708	2220	140	157	19.6	5.0
4.75	0.0784	1900	127	149	17.7	4.75
4.5	0.0874	1620	114	141	15.9	4.5
4.25	0.0980	1360	101	134	14.2	4.25
4.0	0.111	1140	89.8	126	12.6	4.0
3.75	0.126	936	79.0	118	11.0	3.75
3.5	0.144	761	68.8	110	9.62	3.5
3.25	0.168	609	59.3	102	8.30	3.15
3.0	0.197	479	50.5	94.2	7.07	3.0
2.8	0.226	390	44.0	88.0	6.16	2.8
2.5	0.282	277	35.1	78.5	4.91	2.5
2.25	0.350	202	28.4	70.7	3.98	2.25
2.0	0.442	142	22.5	62.8	3.14	2.0
1.9	0.490	122	20.3	59.7	2.84	1.9
1.8	0.546	104	18.2	56.5	2.54	1.8
1.7	0.612	87.2	16.2	53.4	2.27	1.7
1.6	0.691	72.7	14.4	50.3	2.01	1.6
1.5	0.787	59.9	12.6	47.1	1.77	1.5
1.4	0.903	48.7	11.0	44.0	1.54	1.4
1.3	1.05	39.0	9.49	40.8	1.33	1.3
1.2	1.23	30.7	8.09	37.7	1.13	1.2
1.1	1.46	23.6	6.79	34.6	0.950	1.1
1.0	1.77	17.8	5.62	31.4	0.785	1.0

Kanthal A-1 wire

To obtain resistivity at working temperature multiply by the factor C_t in the following table:

°C	20	100	200	300	400	500	600	700	800	900	1000	1100	1200	1300	1400
C_t	1.00	1.00	1.00	1.00	1.00	1.01	1.01	1.02	1.02	1.03	1.04	1.04	1.04	1.04	1.05

Diameter mm	Resistance Ω/m 20°C	cm²/Ω 20°C	Weight g/m	Surface area cm²/m	Cross sectional area mm²	Diameter mm
12.0	0.0128	29400	803	377	113	12.0
10.0	0.0185	17000	558	314	78.5	10.0
9.5	0.0205	14600	503	298	70.9	9.5
8.25	0.0271	9560	380	259	53.5	8.25
8.0	0.0288	8710	357	251	50.3	8.0
7.5	0.0328	7180	314	236	44.2	7.5
7.0	0.0377	5840	273	220	38.5	7.0
6.5	0.0437	4670	236	204	33.2	6.5
6.0	0.0513	3680	201	188	28.3	6.0
5.5	0.0610	2830	169	173	23.8	5.5
5.0	0.0738	2130	139	157	19.6	5.0
4.75	0.0818	1820	126	149	17.7	4.75
4.5	0.0912	1550	113	141	15.9	4.5
4.25	0.102	1310	101	134	14.2	4.25
4.0	0.115	1090	89.2	126	12.6	4.0
3.75	0.131	897	78.4	118	11.0	3.75
3.5	0.151	730	68.3	110	9.62	3.5
3.25	0.175	584	58.9	102	8.30	3.25
3.0	0.205	459	50.2	94.2	7.07	3.0
2.75	0.244	354	42.2	86.4	5.94	2.75
2.5	0.295	266	34.9	78.5	4.91	2.5
2.25	0.365	194	28.2	70.7	3.98	2.25
2.0	0.462	136	22.3	62.8	3.14	2.0
1.8	0.570	99.2	18.1	56.5	2.54	1.8
1.7	0.639	83.6	16.1	53.4	2.27	1.7
1.6	0.721	69.7	14.3	50.3	2.01	1.6
1.5	0.821	59.7	12.5	47.1	1.77	1.5
1.4	0.942	46.7	10.9	44.0	1.54	1.4
1.3	1.09	37.4	9.42	40.8	1.33	1.3
1.2	1.28	29.4	8.03	37.7	1.13	1.2
1.1	1.53	22.6	6.75	34.6	0.950	1.1
1.0	1.85	17.0	5.58	31.4	0.785	1.0

Temperature Conversion Table

The number in the ↓ column indicate the temperatures as read. Conversion to Fahrenheit is given on the right and to Celsius on the left

°C	↓	°F	°C	↓	°F	°C	↓	°F	°C	↓	°F	°C	↓	°F
−17.8	0	32	349	660	1220	738	1360	2480	1127	2060	3740	1516	2760	5000
−12.2	10	50.0	354	670	1238	743	1370	2498	1132	2070	3758	1521	2770	5018
−6.67	20	68.0	360	680	1256	749	1380	2516	1138	2080	3776	1527	2780	5036
−1.11	30	86.0	366	690	1274	754	1390	2534	1143	2090	3794	1532	2790	5054
4.44	40	104.0	371	700	1292	760	1400	2552	1149	2100	3812	1538	2800	5072
10.0	50	122.0	377	710	1310	766	1410	2570	1154	2110	3830	1543	2810	5090
15.6	60	140.0	382	720	1328	771	1420	2588	1160	2120	3848	1549	2820	5108
21.1	70	158.0	388	730	1346	777	1430	2606	1166	2130	3866	1554	2830	5126
26.7	80	176.0	393	740	1364	782	1440	2624	1171	2140	3884	1560	2840	5144
32.2	90	194.0	399	750	1382	788	1450	2624	1177	2150	3902	1566	2850	5162
			404	760	1400	793	1460	2660	1182	2160	3920	1571	2860	5180
			410	770	1418	799	1470	2678	1188	2170	3938	1577	2870	5198
			416	780	1436	804	1480	2696	1193	2180	3956	1582	2880	5216
38	100	212	421	790	1454	810	1490	2714	1199	2190	3974	1588	2890	5234
43	110	230	427	800	1472	816	1500	2732	1204	2200	3992	1593	2900	5252
49	120	248	432	810	1490	821	1510	2750	1210	2210	4010	1599	2910	5270
54	130	266	438	820	1508	827	1520	2768	1216	2220	4028	1604	2920	5288
60	140	284	443	830	1526	832	1530	2786	1221	2230	4046	1610	2930	5036
66	150	302	449	840	1544	838	1540	2804	1227	2240	4064	1616	2940	5324
71	160	320	454	850	1562	843	1550	2822	1232	2250	4082	1621	2950	5342
77	170	338	460	860	1580	849	1560	2840	1238	2260	4100	1627	2960	5360
82	180	356	468	870	1598	854	1570	2858	1243	2270	4118	1632	2970	5376
88	190	374	471	880	1616	860	1580	2876	1249	2280	4138	1638	2980	6396
93	200	392	477	890	1634	866	1590	2894	1254	2290	4154	1643	2990	5414
99	210	410	482	900	1652	871	1600	2912	1260	2300	4172	1649	3000	5432
100	212	413	488	910	1670	877	1610	2930	1266	2310	4190			
104	220	428	493	920	1688	882	1620	2948	1271	2320	4208			
110	230	446	499	930	1706	888	1630	2966	1277	2330	4226			
116	240	464	504	940	1724	893	1640	2984	1282	2340	4244			
121	250	482	510	950	1742	899	1650	3002	1288	2350	4262			
127	260	500	516	960	1760	904	1660	3020	1293	2360	4280			
132	270	518	521	970	1778	910	1670	3038	1299	2370	4298			
138	280	536	527	980	1796	916	1680	3058	1304	2380	4316			
143	290	554	532	990	1814	921	1690	3074	1310	2390	4334			
149	300	572	538	1000	1832	927	1700	3092	1316	2400	4352			
154	310	590	543	1010	1850	932	1710	3110	1321	2410	4370			
160	320	608	549	1020	1868	938	1720	3128	1327	2420	4388			
166	330	626	554	1030	1886	943	1730	3146	1332	2430	4406			
171	340	644	560	1040	1904	949	1740	3164	1338	2440	4424			
177	350	662	566	1050	1922	954	1750	3182	1343	2450	4442			
182	360	680	571	1060	1940	960	1760	3200	1349	2460	4460			
188	370	698	577	1070	1958	966	1770	3218	1354	2470	4478			
193	380	716	582	1080	1976	971	1780	3236	1360	2480	4496			
199	390	734	588	1090	1994	977	1790	3254	1366	2490	4514			
204	400	752	593	1100	2012	982	1800	3272	1371	2500	4532			
210	410	770	599	1110	2030	988	1810	3290	1377	2510	4550			
216	420	788	604	1120	2048	993	1820	3308	1382	2520	4568			
221	430	806	610	1130	2066	999	1830	3326	1388	2530	4586			
227	440	824	616	1140	2084	1004	1840	3344	1393	2540	4604			
232	450	842	621	1150	2102	1010	1850	3362	1399	2550	4622			
238	460	860	627	1160	2120	1016	1860	3380	1404	2560	4640			
243	470	878	632	1170	2138	1021	1870	3398	1410	2570	4658			
249	480	896	638	1180	2156	1027	1880	3416	1416	2580	4676			
254	490	914	643	1190	2174	1032	1890	3434	1421	2590	4694			
260	500	932	649	1200	2192	1038	1900	3452	1427	2600	4712			
266	510	950	654	1210	2210	1043	1910	3470	1432	2610	4730			
271	520	968	660	1220	2228	1049	1920	3488	1438	2620	4748			
277	530	986	666	1230	2246	1054	1930	3056	1443	2630	4766			
282	540	1004	671	1240	2264	1060	1940	3524	1449	2640	4784			
288	550	1022	677	1250	2282	1066	1950	3542	1454	2650	4802			
293	560	1040	682	1260	2300	1071	1960	3560	1460	2660	4820			
299	570	1058	688	1270	2318	1077	1970	3578	1466	2670	4838			
304	580	1076	693	1280	2336	1082	1980	3596	1471	2680	4856			
310	590	1094	699	1290	2354	1088	1990	3614	1477	2690	4874			
316	600	1112	704	1300	2372	1093	2000	3632	1482	2700	4892			
321	610	1130	710	1310	2390	1099	2010	3650	1488	2710	4910			
327	620	1148	716	1320	2408	1104	2020	3668	1493	2720	4928			
332	630	1166	721	1330	2426	1110	2030	3686	1499	2730	4946			
338	640	1184	727	1340	2444	1116	2040	3704	1504	2740	4964			
343	650	1202	732	1350	2462	1121	2050	3722	1510	2750	4982			

INTERPOLATION TABLE

°C		°F
0.56	1	1.8
1.11	2	3.6
1.67	3	5.4
2.22	4	7.2
2.78	5	9.0
3.33	6	10.8
3.89	7	12.6
4.44	8	14.4
5.00	9	16.2
5.56	10	18.0

Suppliers list

Kiln Manufacturers – UK

Bricesco Ltd, Rowhurst Close, Chesterton, Newcastle, Staffs.

Potclay Kilns Ltd, Brickkiln Lane, Etruria, Stoke-on-Trent.

Potterycrafts Ltd. Campbell Road, Stoke-on-Trent.

Kilns & Furnaces Ltd, Keele Street, Tunstall, Stoke-on-Trent.

Stanton Pottery Supplies Ltd, Canal Lane, Westport Lake, Tunstall, Stoke-on-Trent.

Drayton Kiln Co Ltd, Plantation Road, Newstead Industrial Estate, Trentham, Stoke-on-Trent.

Cromartie Kilns Ltd, Parkhall Road, Weston Coyney, Stoke-on-Trent.

Catterson Smith, RM., Ltd, Woodrolfe Road, Maldon, Essex

Kiln Manufacturers – USA/Canada

American Art Clay Co. Inc., 4717 W 16 Street, Indianapolis IN 46222

Olympic Kilns, 4225 Thurmond Tanner Road, Flowery Branch, GA 30542

Evenheat Kiln Inc., 6949 Legion Road, Caseville, MI 48725

Cress Mfg Co Inc., 1718 Floradale Ave, S.E1 Monte CA91733

Skutt Ceramic Products, 2618 SE Steele Street, Portland OR 97202.

Bailey Ceramic Supply, PO 1577 Kingston, NY 12401.

Aim Kilns, 369 Main St, Ramona, CA 92065.

Paragon Industries, PO Box 85808, Mesquite TX 75185–0808

L&L Mfg Co., Box 938, Chester, PA 19016.

Mercedes Ceramic Supplies, 30 Wallace Street, Woodbridge, Ontario, Canada.

Refractory Materials

Thermal Ceramics Ltd, Tebay Rd, Bromborough, Wirral, Merseyside.

Micropore Insulation Ltd, 1 Arrowe Brook Road, Upton, Wirral

Skamol a/s, 10 Water Street, Newcastle, Staffs.

Studweldpro-UK Ltd, Old Hall Lane, East Markham, Newark, Notts.

Hepworth Refractories Ltd, Genefax House, Tapton Park, Sheffield.

Steetley Refractories Ltd, Steetley Works, Worksop, Notts.

Element wire

Kanthal AB, PO Box 502 73427 Hallstahammar, Sweden

Resistalloy Ltd, Riverside Works, Weedon Street, Sheffield

General Suppliers, firing accessories etc

Potclays Ltd, Brickkiln Lane, Etruria, Stoke-on-Trent.

Taylor Tunnicliffe Ltd, Uttoxeter Road, Longton, Stoke-on-Trent.

Medcol Ltd, Unit 17, Woods Browning Ind. Estate, Bodmin, Cornwall.

Potterycrafts, Campbell Road, Stoke-on-Trent

Reward Europe Ltd, Unit 10 Brookhouse Ind. Est. Cheadle, Stoke-on-Trent.

Bath Potters Supply, 2 Dorset Place, Bath.

Scarva Pottery Supplies, Unit 20 Scarva Road Industrial Est., Banbridge, Co. Down, N. Ireland

Stanton Pottery Supplies, Canal Lane, Westport Lake, Tunstall, Stoke-on-Trent.

Edward Orton Jr Ceramic Foundation, 6991 Old 3C Hwy, Westerville, OH 43081.

Bell Research Inc., 157 Virginia Avenue, Chester WV 26034.

American Art Clay Co Inc. 4717 W 16th St, Indianapolis IN 46222.

Laguna Clay, 14400 Lomitas Ave, City of Industry, CA 91746.

National Artcraft Co, 23456 Mercantile Road, Beachwood OH 44122.

Index